SHEM FLEENOR

Fighting for the Enlightenment:

American Volunteers' Spanish War
Correspondence

1848 Publishing Company

New York and Melbourne

ISBN: 978-1-951231-01-9

Table of Contents

Prologue

"The War in Spain, 1936 – 1939: Causes and Combatants" 3

Introduction

.... 38

Chapter One

"Psychology, Ideology, Idealism, and The Will to Fight Fascism in the Great Depression" 44

Chapter Two

"Scholars, Artists and Idealists" 63

Chapter Three

"Communism in the Great Depression" 77

Chapter Four

"The Longue Durée of Revolutions from Enlightenment to Spain" 98

Chapter Five

"Volunteers for Liberty" 118

Chapter Six

"Volunteers for Equality"... 138

Chapter Seven

"Volunteers for Fraternity" 164

Epilogue 198

Prologue

"The War in Spain, 1936 – 1939:

Causes and Combatants"

Spain was a constitutional monarchy through most of the nineteenth century. But in 1873 King Amadeo I abdicated his throne due to increasing political pressure, giving rise to the First Spanish Republic. In Spain – as was the case in most of Europe – ideas spawned by the Enlightenment in the previous century put pressure on monarchies and their colonial empires around the world. Spain, a global empire in rapid recession, was central to a rising tide of anti-colonialist sentiment spawned by Enlightenment ideas, which helped, in part, the United States push the Spanish Crown out of North America and the Pacific at the beginning of the twentieth century after the Spanish Crown's long and bitter fight with rebels in Cuba and the Philippines.

The unraveling of the Spanish empire and squabbles between factions of monarchists, coupled with the Great Depression, helped set the stage for what seemed to be a new dawn of democracy and economic reform in Spain. Soon after the establishment of Spain's Second Republic in 1931, a plot was hatched by military leaders, monarchists, and the clergy to topple it. But when Prime Minister Niceto Alcalá-Zamora's government did not take decisive action against the liberal forces primarily responsible for the rise of the

Second Republic, the plan was scuttled – for a while, anyway.[1]

The constitution of 1931 had revolutionary elements when compared to the ancient regime; it enfranchised former wards of the state – peasants and women – by providing universal suffrage. Fearing a greater recession of power due to the enfranchisement of women and peasants sponsored by centrists, together with the Agrarian Law of 1932, former elites were increasingly alienated, especially by the distribution of land to poor peasants, many of whom toiled under slave-like conditions while many landowners lived most of the year on the French Riviera. Millions of Spaniards had been living in poverty under the firm control of aristocratic landowners in a quasi-feudal system for hundreds of years.

Spain's economic productivity, despite being an empire, also lagged far behind other industrial nations such as England, France, Russia and the United States. Reforms designed to redress the pervasive economic and social inequity in 1930s Spain drew especially strong opposition from landowners and aristocrats. At the same time, the anti-clericalist acts of the Second Republic made powerful enemies of many clergymen because it nullified special privileges the Catholic Church had been entitled to for centuries. Cutbacks in military spending also alienated many elements of Spain's Armed Forces,

---

[1] Hank Rubin, foreword by Peter N. Carroll, *Spain's Cause Was Mine: A Memoir of an American Medic in the Spanish Civil War* (Carbondale, Southern Illinois University Press, 1997).

putting powerful leaders, accustomed to privilege, in an increasingly defensive position in contrast to the nation's poor who were increasingly in league with progressive-minded centrists and liberals dedicated to fostering a greater degree of social equality amongst the Spanish peasantry and traditional economic and political powerbrokers.[2]

But by the 1933 parliamentary elections many of Spain's conservatives had used their political and economic clout to regain a balance of power. And between 1933 and 1935 the country was rocked by vigilante violence, especially in cities such as Barcelona, Madrid, and Valencia where there were influential militia's controlled by leftist labor unions. In February 1936, a coalition of leftwing groups known as the Popular Front (which included liberal Republicans, Socialists, and a small Communist Party, but not the Anarchists (who formally rejected cooperation) won closely-contested parliamentary elections. The military, which was led by General Francisco Franco, and supported by anti-Republican leaders and Falangists, began conspiring for armed insurrection to ensure the final defeat of the democratically elected Popular Front government. During the spring of 1936 street fighting between conservative and leftist factions erupted spontaneously in cities throughout the nation; public violence took various forms, including political assassinations and church burnings by anarchist groups.

The killing of José Calvo Sotelo, a prominent member of parliament stoked hysteria among

---

[2] Ronald Frasier, *Blood of Spain: An Oral History of the Spanish Civil War*, (New York, Pimlico, 1994) 38-39.

conservatives who argued that the murder especially demonstrated the need for a restoration of law and order throughout Spain.[3] Although the conservative Nationalist generals were already in the advanced stages of a planned uprising, Sotelo's murder provided a convenient pretext, rationale, catalyst and justification for their coup.[4]

In the years preceding the killing of Sotelo, however, there was widespread instability in Spain's parliamentary government. The conservatives that regained the balance of political power in the 1933 elections regarded reform as an aggressive challenge to their historical privilege and therefore unraveled many reform measures instituted after the monarchies' ouster in 1931. In 1933 a conservative dictatorship rolled back reforms and began restoring traditional property rights to owners who had been forced to relinquish land to their peasants. In addition to being incredibly corrupt, the Army's officer corps was also an incredibly top-heavy institution; one officer on average oversaw twelve men. Eight thousand military officers who refused to swear allegiance to the democratically elected Popular Front government that rose to power in February 1936 were retired (with full pay), which helped further sow the seeds for the military coup. Widespread restructuring of traditional power relations helped trigger backlash throughout Spain and lurched the country closer to war.

---

[3] Hugh Thomas, *The Spanish Civil War* (New York, Random House, 2001) 196–198 and 309.

[4] Anthony Beevor, *The Battle for Spain: The Spanish Civil War 1936 – 1939* (London, Penguin, 1982) 49.

The rollback of social reforms by the dictatorship that lasted from 1933 to 1936, ironically, pushed the pendulum back to the left of center. "Despite corruption of the ballot, and the constant terrorism of the Army, the landlords and industrialists, despite the fulminations of the Catholic Church," American volunteer Alvah Bessie noted in 1939, "the Popular Front won the elections of February 1936 by an overwhelming majority."[5] But when some democratic changes were undertaken in the Army, which was widely considered as oppressive as the ancient regime monarchy that was deposed in 1931, Army officials such as Franco grew increasingly determined to topple the Republic by any means necessary.

The Coup

On July 17, 1936, the militarist plotters signaled the beginning of the coup by broadcasting, "Over all of Spain, the sky is clear" across radio waves. Two British MI6 intelligence agents, Cecil Bebb and Major Hugh Pollard, then flew Franco to Spanish Morocco, where he met with co-conspirator, Juan March Ordinas. In Morocco, Franco and Ordinas readied the Spanish Army of Africa, comprised primarily of Muslim Moors, to invade Spain.[6] The regular army on the Iberian Peninsula meanwhile rose in rebellion. Franco's forces anticipated a swift victory. But the Republicans, with their tremendous human resources of the People's

---

[5] Alvah Bessie, *Men in Battle: A Story of Americans in Spain*, (New York, Scribner, 1939), 346, 347, 348. Bessie went to Spain when he was 33 years, and had moderate successes as a novelist and screenwriter before being blacklisted during the McCarthyism.

[6] Michael Alpert, *BBC History Magazine* April 2002.

Army, also anticipated no great difficulty in containing the coup. Notwithstanding that fierce fighting spread from the garrison centers of the protectorate of Morocco to every province and major city on the Spanish mainland, the capital city of Madrid was not taken by the Nationalists, which helped ensure a long and bitter battle for the control of Spain.

Meanwhile in Berlin, Germany, Adolf Hitler was preparing to showcase the Third Reich's cultural prowess at the 1936 Olympics; Benito Mussolini's fully industrialized army was engaged in a war with Ethiopian agrarians. In Geneva, Switzerland, at the assembly of the League of Nations, Ethiopian emperor Haile Selassie denounced the Italians' invasion of his country and the use of poison gas against his people. From the Vatican, in Italy, Pope Pius XII, a supporter of Mussolini's regime, published an encyclical banning motion pictures for spreading evil.

Hitler and Mussolini quickly recognized the legitimacy of Franco's regime and began aiding the Nationalists. As many as 19,000 Germans fought in Spain; 6,000 of whom were members of the notorious Condor Legion, Hitler's state-of-the-art air and armored special force. In total, Nazi Germany provided Franco's Nationalists with 600 planes, 200 tanks, and 1,000 artillery pieces. The Italian Corto Troupe Volontarie (CTV) reached a high of about 50,000 men during the Spanish War and, by rotation, more than 75,000 Italians fought for the Nationalists in Spain. Fascist Italy also provided the Spanish Nationalists with 660 planes, 150 tanks and 1,000 artillery pieces. [7] Many of Italy's

---

[7] Thomas, 944.

"volunteers" came directly from Ethiopia. Franco's Nationalist rebels were also allied with António de Oliveira Salazar's Portugal, whose nation provided resources and sanctuary.[8]

All these forces, together with massive armament and material aid, were used over a period of two and a half years against a blockaded and largely starving Republic whose government had been democratically elected. It was clear to most combatants on the ground that the purpose of the axis alliance with the Spanish rebels was the extermination of democracy in Spain as the first step toward an all-out war for the extermination of democracy in Europe, and ultimately the quashing of egalitarian ideals central to the Enlightenment – especially liberty, equality and fraternity.

Insofar as the rebellion had been plotted with the aid of the governments of Berlin and Rome, the Spanish War was later considered "the opening guns of World War II."[9] The war in Spain ultimately lasted from July 17, 1936 to April 1, 1939 – far longer than either side had anticipated. Like all so-called civil wars, it was bitterly fought. Brother fought brother, some nuns and priests were murdered for providing sanctuary to Nationalists, and sometimes for revenge. But what was especially unique about the Spanish War is how global

---

[8] John Tisa, *Recalling the Good Fight: An Autobiography of the Spanish Civil War*, (South Hadley, Mass.: Bergin & Garvey Publishers, Inc., 1985) 21. Poland the fascist legions of General Pilsudski had overthrown the Republic headed by Paderewski; Metaxis had created a dictatorship in Greece.

[9] F. Jay Taylor, *The United States and the Spanish Civil War* (New York, Bookman, 1956) xi and 18.

its implications were. In fact, it is a misnomer to refer to the war between Franco's Nationalists and the Republic of Spain as a civil war at all, considering the combatants were from all around the world.

"You have made a mistake in the April 5 issue of the *Clarion*," American volunteer Sidney Rosenblatt wrote a friend back home in 1938. "You state that there is a 'Civil War in Spain.' This is incorrect... It is a war of international Fascist aggression."[10] Lincoln Battalion commander, Robert Merriman, an economist trained at the University of California at Berkeley, likewise decried the notion that the Spanish War was a civil war, a description he felt Hitler and Mussolini used to deceive England, France, and the U.S. into positions of neutrality. "The free countries must go to the aid of the Spanish Republic not only to support freedom," Merriman explained to his wife, "but also because Hitler and Mussolini were violating neutrality anyway by sending to Franco thousands of troops, planes and tanks."[11] To refer to the war in Spain from July 1936 to 1939 as a "civil war" is thus a misnomer. Combatants were aware that Spain was the beginning of a new world war seemingly long before the heads of state of the

---

[10] Sidney Rosenblatt letter to Estelle, May 19, 1938, from Socorro Rojo, Albacete, Spain. Socorro Rojo Internacional (SRI), International Red Aid, took the place of the Red Cross in Republican Spain. Rosenblatt Papers, ALBA.261, Tamiment Library/Robert F. Wagner Labor Archives. Elmer Holmes Tamiment Library, 70 Washington Square South, New York NY 10012, New York University Libraries.

[11] Marion Merriman and Warren Lerude, *American Commander in Spain: Robert Hale Merriman and the Abraham Lincoln Brigade* (Reno, University of Nevada Press, 1986) 69.

western empires – The U.S., England, and France – were willing or able to believe.

The Misguided Myth of Neutrality

The Spanish War that lasted officially from 1936 to 1939 was part of a broadly-based global cross-class struggle that should have, in theory, united all the western democracies alongside the Spanish Republic, but the great democracies of the world – France, England, and the United States -- were also industrialized empires whose politicians were often more concerned about their own economic and political interests than they were with defending Spain's democratically elected government. Even progressives in France, England and the U.S, were wary of the prospect of being pulled into another world war.

By August 1936, a month after the coup, the "non-intervention" policy of the major European powers – France and England -- left the Republic almost entirely dependent on the Soviet Union for supplies of arms and materials. Russian Premier Josef Stalin, fearing an invasion of the Ukraine by Hitler's Wehrmacht, reluctantly sent supplies and between 2,000 to 3,000 military advisors to aid Spain in exchange for Spanish gold in the hope of opening a proxy-eastern front in a war he believed inevitable with Germany. In total, the USSR provided Spain with 806 planes, 362 tanks, and 1,555 artillery pieces – a scant amount compared to the aid sent to Franco by Hitler and Mussolini.[12] And so the

---

[12] It is also important to note that by 1937 the Soviet Union was also increasingly preoccupied with a war in China, which had been invaded by Japanese Fascists. Many Russians still very much remembered a long and bitter war fought against the Japanese during the first decade of the twentieth

Soviet Union, like Germany and Italy, simply ignored the League of Nations' embargo and sold arms to the Republic. The Soviets were the Republic's only important source of major weapons. The Spanish Republic, it should be noted, was not, however, a Communist or Socialist state, but it did welcome any aid -- organized or otherwise – from any source willing to provide it.[13] Since the Republic was not aided by England, France or the U.S., it was faced with a catch-22: acquiesce to the Nationalists or ally itself with Stalin.

The Republic had inferior resources because they were not aided by western democracies, as even the aid provided by the Soviet Union was antiquated compared to the weaponry and manpower provided to Hitler by Franco and Mussolini. Most of the weapons and artillery sent to Spain were antiques because Stalin did not want the arms to be traced back to the Soviet Union. He also used weapons captured from past conflicts.[14] In other words, although Stalin was aiding Spain, he was ultimately preparing for a showdown with Hitler in Russia that he rightly believed to be inevitable. So, Stalin kept his best firepower and men at home. Additionally, transporting weaponry was complicated, especially after Spain was blockaded by the

---

century. Academy of Sciences of the USSR, *International Solidarity with the Spanish Republic, 1936-1939* (Moscow: Progress, 1974), 329-30.

[13] Hank Rubin, foreword by Peter N. Carroll, *Spain's Cause Was Mine: A Memoir of an American Medic in the Spanish Civil War* (Carbondale, Southern Illinois University Press, 1997), 19.

[14] Gerald Howson, *Arms for Spain* (New York: St. Martin's Press, 1998).

British Navy, and eventually even the modest flow of arms from Russia to Spain "slowed to a trickle."[15]

France, under the Socialist Leon Blum, indicated some interest in allowing material aid to Spain, but dared not oppose the British and risk being left alone to face Mussolini and Hitler. England's Prime Minister, Neville Chamberlain, especially wanted to avoid conflict with Germany and Italy. Both empires, along with Italy and Germany, signed "Non-intervention" agreements prohibiting the sale of arms to either side of the conflict and instead established an impotent international committee to monitor compliance – which was ultimately ignored openly by Hitler and Mussolini and secretively by Stalin. As Mussolini said soon after

---

[15] While Soviet troops amounted to no more than 700 men, Soviet "volunteers" often operated Soviet-made Republican tanks and aircraft, while the Spanish People's Army and International volunteers mostly comprised the front lines in battles versus Fascist forces. James Neugrass, introduction by Peter Carroll, *War is Beautiful: An American Ambulance Driver in the Spanish Civil War* (New York, The New Press, 2008). In 1937, Isidore James Neugass, a poet and novelist praised in the *New York Times*, joined nearly 3,000 other passionate young Americans who traveled to Spain as part of the Abraham Lincoln Battalion. He was born in New Orleans, January 29, 1905 into a well-to-do Jewish family. He began writing as a teenager. He attended Yale, Harvard, and Oxford and worked as a book reviewer, shoe salesman, social worker, and fencing coach before shipping off to Spain when he was 32 to be an ambulance driver for the American Medical Bureau to Save Spanish Democracy. Although rumors persisted over the years that Neugass had written a memoir, the manuscript did not come to light for sixty years, until a bookseller discovered it among papers in a New England house once occupied by the radical critic and editor Max Eastman.

Franco's forces triumphed, "we intervened from the first to the last moment."[16]

By the end of 1936 it was clear to everyone that if Britain had aided the Spanish Government, even to the extent of supplying a few million dollars' worth of arms, Franco's regime would have quickly collapsed and the Germans' strategy would have been severely hampered.[17] Instead, the French government cooperated with the aggressors by choking off its border crossings along the Pyrenees and southern seaports in the hopes of preventing volunteers sympathetic to the Republic from entering the fray.[18]

Although mired in the Great Depression, the U.S. was far more economically and politically stable compared to the widespread poverty and political turmoil that helped usher in the era of fascism in Western Europe, but the U.S. had a policy of isolation since the end of the World War, and helped establish the League of Nations in part to avoid European conflicts. Also, many U.S. politicians and officials wanted to stay neutral because they saw the Popular Front in Spain as a stalking-horse for the Soviet Union and they had a greater affinity and affiliation with Fascists, who were devout capitalists. It is also important to point out that by the 1937 show trials in Moscow it was increasingly

---

[16] Arthur H. Landis, *The Abraham Lincoln Brigade* (New York, Citadel Press, 1967) xviii.

[17] George Orwell, "Looking back on the Spanish War" (London, New Road, 1943).

[18] John Tisa, *Recalling the Good Fight: An Autobiography of the Spanish Civil War*, (South Hadley, Mass.: Bergin & Garvey Publishers, Inc., 1985) 21.

apparent to many devoted idealists that the Communist Party's high moral proclamations were a sham.[19] The Republic, some also criticized, did not appear to represent the American capitalist values of free enterprise. American corporations had $80 million invested in Spain, mostly the ITT telegraphs and telephones enterprises. ITT, together with the Spanish subsidiaries of Ford and GM, was taken over by a trade-union militia at the outbreak of the war in Spain, which

---

[19] The show trials of the mid-1930s expose the fact that Stalin had abandoned the Marxist principles advocated by Vladimir Lenin and Leon Trotsky, most notably the notion that a socialist revolution was possible only on a global (not nationalist) scale. Though Stalin increasingly betrayed telltale signs of being a madman, his mania was rooted in legitimate fears of invasion by Fascists on either side of the Soviet Union. Russia had, it is important to note, fought a bitter war with Japan in the first decade of the twentieth century and with Germany a decade after. It is also important to note that Stalin was inundated with enemies – both real and imagined – inside and surrounding Russia. The Soviets were actually aiding a Republic defending itself from Fascist counter-revolutionaries on one hand, and waging a quasi-war with Trotskyist anarchist revolutionaries inside Spain and around the world.[19] By the start of the coup in Spain in July 1936 Stalin was increasingly surrounded by enemies – ultra conservative fascists throughout Europe and Asia, but also anarchists in Spain, as well as Trotskyists in Russia and throughout the world who increasingly criticized him for diverging from the Marxist and Leninist principles that defined the Russian Revolution fought between the Leftist Reds and Monarchial Whites two decades earlier. Gerald Howson, Arms for Spain (New York: St. Martin's Press, 1998). See also Edward Rothstein, "The Spanish Civil War: Black and White in a Murky, Ambiguous World: Facing Fascism: New York and the Spanish Civil War - Exhibition – Review," The New York Times, 3, 24, 2007.

ultimately helped American corporations, such as Texaco, justify aiding Franco.[20]

Before volunteers sailed for France en route to Spanish battlefields and trenches, Alfred Phillips, a Representative for the state of Connecticut, offered a resolution that would deprive any and all Americans who defied official United States neutrality laws of "all rights and privileges of citizenship." Not only were American passports invalidated for travel in Spain, but American officials in Spain were also instructed to not extend protection or assistance to Americans who had defied their own government in order to aid the Spanish Republic.[21] In the interwar age of American isolationism, the willingness of volunteers to risk life, limb and citizenship especially demonstrates their idealism, but it also demonstrates the lack of idealism amongst U.S. politicians, especially in contrast to the nearly three thousand Americans who defied federal law to aid the Spanish Republic against fascism.

On August 11, 1936 the U.S. announced a "moral embargo" on arms supplies to Spain. Following the embargo, the state department marked U.S. passports with "not valid for Spain" and demanded that all citizens proposing to travel abroad furnish an affidavit that they were not bound for Spain. The Roosevelt White House, however, was somewhat sympathetic to the Republic and permitted Ernest Hemingway and war correspondent Martha Gellhorn,

---

[20] Michael Alpert, *A New International History of the Spanish Civil War* (New York, Palgrave Macmillan, 1994) 109.

[21] F. Jay Taylor, *The United States and the Spanish Civil War* (New York, Bookman, 1956) 108.

who had recently returned from Spain, to hold a private exhibition at the White House of a pro-Republican documentary film, *The Spanish Earth*. During the screening the president reportedly sighed as he said, "Spain is the vicarious sacrifice for all of us."[22]

President's Roosevelt's idealism in regards to Spain was, however, bound by realpolitick associated with bad memories of the World War concluded less than two decades before, which helped shape and mold the nations' foreign policies during the Great Depression. Roosevelt's sympathies for the Republic and weariness of fascism aside, powerful forces in Congress and throughout the body politic prevented his administration from intervening. During the November 1936 cycle, which was just ten weeks after the coup began, Roosevelt's Democratic majority, many of whom were from the Fascistic Jim Crow South, strongly opposed support for Spain's Popular Front government. And so the U.S.'s official policy was neutrality, which "pleased only the least liberal segments of the population."[23]

Adherents of the Republic, however, seemed to think Roosevelt was more an idealist than pragmatist, and continued to appeal to his conscience. "I do not see how they (the Spanish Republicans can lose), unless the

---

[22] Martha Gellhorn to Eleanor Roosevelt [1938], Box 1459, Franklin D. Roosevelt Library, Hyde Park, New York; in Peter N. Carroll & James D. Fernadez, *Facing Fascism: New York & The Spanish Civil War* (New York, NYU Press, 2007) 13 note 4.

[23] Allen Guttmann, *The Wound in the Heart: America and the Spanish Civil War* (New York, The Free Press/Macmillan, 1962) 210.

democracies allow Hitler and Mussolini to continue sending unlimited supplies," war correspondent, Martha Gellhorn, wrote her friend, Eleanor Roosevelt, in a heartfelt letter from Barcelona in the Spring of 1938. "Neither manpower nor ability nor determination are lacking: but it is a fight between Democracy and three fascisms."[24]

Despite Roosevelt's "Quarantine speech" in 1937 and his apparent sympathies for the Republic, a stiffer neutrality law in May 1937 ensured that the U.S. would take a laissez faire approach to the War in Spain.[25] Washington did, however, permit some corporations, such as Texaco, to sell supplies to Franco -- on credit no less. In other words, economic expedience trumped enlightened idealism in the context of an increasingly tangled global market, which ultimately permitted Hitler, Mussolini and Franco to topple Spain's Popular Front government and push the world to the brink of another World War.

<u>The International Brigades</u>

Though France, England, and the U.S.'s state departments' official policy was neutrality, many citizens from the "neutral" nations risked life and, in some cases citizenship, to defend the Spanish Republic from Franco, Hitler and Mussolini's fascist forces. Many non-Spanish people, often affiliated with radical,

---

[24] Martha Gellhorn to Eleanor Roosevelt, April 25 and 25, 1938, Barcelona, Spain.

[25] Michael Alpert, *A New International History of the Spanish Civil War* (New York, Palgrave Macmillan, 1994) 111 - 112.

communist, socialist parties and/or trade unions joined the International Brigades, believing that the Spanish Republic was the front line of the war against fascism throughout the world. Roughly 30,000 foreign nationals from 53 nations fought in the International Brigades. Although many volunteers were Communists, Socialists and/or trade unionists, many others were not.

The first International Brigade volunteers arrived in Madrid in November, 1936, participating in the dramatic defense of the city. Despite volunteers' devotion to their ideals, there were not many members of the International Brigades, who never numbered more than 30,000 in Spain at any one time, and no more than 6,000 in any one military campaign.[26] The Eleventh Brigade was comprised of German-speaking volunteers. The Twelfth was composed of Italian anti-fascists. German anti-fascists formed the Thälmann Battalion, which was named after an imprisoned German Communist; Polish volunteers formed the Dabrowski Battalion, and Italians named themselves the

---

[26] They were comprised of five brigades, nearly 30 battalions, and innumerable support units. German and Italian volunteers, who had confronted fascism in their own countries, formed the hard core of the Brigades. The largest single body of International Brigaders, the French (just under 9,000), overwhelmingly came from the working class (92 per cent) and included no more than 1 per cent students and members of the liberal professions; virtually all of them were communists. These figures are in stark contrast to the American volunteers, many of whom were educated. Eric Hobsbawm, "War of Ideas" *The Guardian*, February 17, 2007. See also Arthur H. Landis, *The Abraham Lincoln Brigade* (New York, Citadel Press, 1967) xvi.

Garibaldis.[27] The Thirteenth Battalion was composed of Slavic-speaking Poles, Czechs, and Eastern Europeans; The Fourteenth was comprised of French and Belgian volunteers. The Fifteenth International Brigade was comprised of English-Speaking volunteers, including Americans. The XVth Brigade included the British Saklavala Battalion, which was named for a Hindu member of Parliament from London. The Canadian Mackenzie-Papineau Battalion was named for a Canadian prime minister, William Lloyd Mackenzie, who, with Louis Papineau, led an armed struggle against the excesses of the British Crown in Canada in 1837. The fourth battalion was the Abraham Lincolns, which was comprised mostly of American volunteers.[28] The Lincoln Battalion was short-lived because the decimated George Washington Battalion combined with the Lincolns and the Canadian Mackenzie-Papineau Battalion.[29]

<u>Demographic Sketch of the American Volunteers</u>

The "average" American volunteer for the Spanish Republic was a man in his twenties who had lived in an industrial or urban center where labor unions and radical political parties had been most active.

---

[27] James Neugrass, introduction by Peter Carroll, *War is Beautiful: An American Ambulance Driver in the Spanish Civil War*, (New York, The New Press, 2008) xiii.

[28] Brigades are composed of battalions. Many refer to the Abraham Lincoln Battalion as Brigade. But it was actually a battalion.

[29] Victor Hoar, "In Our Time: The Abraham Lincoln Brigade and the Historians," *American Quarterly*, Vol. 22, No. 1 (Spring, 1970), pp. 112-119.

Between a fifth and a third of the 2,750 to 3,000 Americans who served in Spain had been born in the New York or had lived there by the time they volunteered.[30] Perhaps as many as one thousand New Yorkers crossed the Atlantic to fight; and at least a third of them never returned. Roughly one third to one half of the American volunteers were killed or wounded in Spain.[31]

Two-thirds of the group were in their twenties, with the median age being 28. Volunteers hailed from every state in the Union save Delaware and Wyoming, and the greatest numbers came from New York, California, Pennsylvania and Illinois. Most American volunteers were born between the Spanish-American War and World War I and lived in urban areas with high immigrant populations. Many of the American volunteers were children of immigrant parents and thus felt a more immediate connection with Europe and Latin America than Anglo-Saxon Americans tended to. There were also a half-dozen Native Americans, two Chinese Americans, one Japanese American, as well as representatives of almost every white ethnic group.

Dozens of women also volunteered, serving as nurses, technicians, ambulance drivers, and truck drivers. The ethnic, racial, gender and class diversity

---

[30] Justin Byrne "From Brooklyn to Belchite: New Yorkers in the Abraham Lincoln Brigade" in Peter N. Carroll & James D. Fernadez, *Facing Fascism: New York & The Spanish Civil War* (New York, NYU Press, 2007) 72 – 75.

[31] Hank Rubin, foreword by Peter N. Carroll, *Spain's Cause Was Mine: A Memoir of an American Medic in the Spanish Civil War* (Carbondale, Southern Illinois University Press, 1997).

among the American volunteers fostered a communitarian and melting pot ideology that dovetailed with the "Popular Front" politics of the Depression era in which liberals, many of whom were united by a fear of fascism, set aside factional and sectarian differences to affirm a shared commitment to progressive, domestic and foreign policies.

Nearly a third to forty percent of the volunteers were Jewish and acutely cognizant that they were fighting a brand of fascism designed, in part, to annihilate their race. Ninety to one-hundred of the volunteers were African Americans whose political consciousness had been shaped by the threat of Ku Klux Klan fascism and/or lynch terrorism. Many African Americans volunteers were likewise compelled to fight fascism as soon as Benito Mussolini invaded Ethiopia and saw the military coup in Spain as an extension of the extermination of Africans.

The Spanish War was the first time in American history in which black soldiers served alongside white infantry as full and equal partners. A Texan turned Chicagoan named Oliver Law, a leader of the unemployment movement during the Great Depression, was a commander of the Lincoln Battalion. He was the first black man to have field command over white Americans in any military conflict.[32]

---

[32] Law was born in Texas October 23, 1900. He joined the U.S. army at the age of 19 and served until he was 25 years old. He was a member of the 24th infantry, a black outfit stationed on the Mexican border. During the Depression he joined the Longshoreman's association and the Works Project Administration. He joined the Communist party in 1932 and was jailed and seriously beaten by Chicago's Red Squad on

Fewer than half the volunteers had any military experience prior to going to Spain, and of those who did most were often trained in the National Guard, rather than regular Army. Only forty-five American volunteers had served in World War I. One volunteer had a wooden leg; another was blind in one eye; some had chronic illnesses like asthma.[33] Many of them worked in factories or on docks in New York, Boston or San Francisco; others were seaman; many of them were college students active in a Popular Front organization such as the League Against War and Fascism. In fact, the two most "productive occupations" amongst the American volunteers were seamen and students. But there was an equal representation of artists and truck drivers.[34] One volunteer resigned his job with the F.B.I. to fight in Spain; another was a motion-picture projectionist, and two of them were vaudeville

---

more than one occasion. Law was one of the first American volunteers for the Spanish Republic. He sailed for Spain aboard the Paris on January 16, 1937. He quickly worked his way up through the ranks and by the summer of 1937 was leading the Lincoln Battalion. On July 10, 1937, the fourth day of the Brunete Offensive he was mortally wounded while leading an assault on the heavily fortified Mosquito Ridge on November 21, 1987, fifty years after his death Law's achievement was recognized by Chicago mayor Harold Washington who declared the day "Oliver Law and Lincoln Brigade Day."

[33] Peter N. Carroll, *The Odyssey of the Abraham Lincoln Brigade: Americans in the Spanish Civil War* (Stanford, CA: Stanford University Press, 1994).

[34] Gary L. Anderson and Kathryn G. Herr, eds. *Encyclopedia of Activism and Social Justice*, Kristen E. Gwinn, "Abraham Lincoln Brigade" (Thousand Oaks, Ca. SAGE Publications, Inc. 2007).

performers; some were newspaper reporters; one man had made his living as a professional wrestler, and another had barnstormed the country as a stunt pilot. In short, there was wide diversity of American volunteers who went to Spain in 1937-38. Though many were members of Communist affiliated organizations, most, including the Communists, were guided to Spain by a sense of idealism they felt was especially threatened by fascism.

Americans in Spain

Americans began arriving in Spain by the dozens early in the winter of 1937. Navigating the steep Pyrenees mountains in the dead of night in the middle of winter, or by crowding cramped fishing boats in the Mediterranean, was especially difficult. Some of the Americans were rounded up and imprisoned by French border police; other volunteers were stopped by non-intervention patrols; a dozen others died when the *Ciudad de Barcelona* was torpedoed. Yet, despite the hazards, nearly 3,000 Americans succeeded in reaching Spain.

After being smuggled into Spain from France, the Americans trained at Villanueva de la Jara – an agricultural town east of Spain's capitol city, Madrid. The American volunteers unanimously voted on the name, the "Lincoln Battalion" in honor of the sixteenth president of the United States, who is widely credited with the abolition of chattel slavery in the U.S. They were housed in an abandoned monastery, of which the walls were adorned with graffiti and slogans such as "Viva La Republica," "No Pasaran," and "Down with

Fascism" left by French troops who stayed there before the Americans arrived.[35]

Training was initially hampered by wintry weather and lack of resources, such as weapons and bullets. Resources were so limited that the American volunteers were only permitted to fire five rounds of ammo into a hillside before being sent into combat.[36]

---

[35] John Tisa, *Recalling the Good Fight: An Autobiography of the Spanish Civil War* (South Hadley, Mass.: Bergin & Garvey Publishers, Inc., 1985) 25. Tisa was one of the first Americans to arrive in Spain. He was also probably one of the last to leave, except for Prisoners of War held after the fall of the Republic. He was in Spain from January 1937 to February 1939. In the Spring of 1938, he became the editor of Volunteer For Liberty, succeeding Edwin Rolfe. He was born April 6, 1914, in Philadelphia, Pennsylvania. He was of Cuban and Italian ancestry. He attended Brockwood Labor College and was a member of the CP and an organizer for the YCL.

[36] Edwin Rolfe, *The Lincoln Battalion* (New York, Random House, 1939), 4. Rolfe was born Solomon Fishman to Russian Jewish parents. He spent the first few years of his life in Philadelphia before the family moved to New York City. His father was a socialist and official of a union local in New York. He later became a member of the Lovestonite faction of the Communist Party. His mother was active in the birth control movement, a supporter of the striking Paterson silk workers in 1913, and a member of the Communist Party. During high school, Fishman began using pen names, using the name Edwin Rolfe on some publications in the 1920s. Rolfe joined the Party in 1925 when he was 15 and was assigned to the Young Communist League. He published his first poem, "The Ballad of the Subway Digger," in the Daily Worker in 1927. He quit the Party in 1929 and moved from New York City to Madison, Wisconsin, to enroll in the Experimental College at the University of Wisconsin at Madison. He spent his time writing non-political poems between 1929 and 1930 and in 1932 was published in Pagany. He left the university during his second year and rejoined the Party in New York City. After a variety of temporary jobs, he began working full time at the Daily Worker. Rolfe published To My Contemporaries, his first

When the battalion was finally complete, it consisted of two infantry companies of three sections each, a machine gun company named in honor of abolitionist John Brown, a first aid and medical section (which included a well-trained first aid unit from Holland), a kitchen staff attached to the supply and transport department, an armory section, and a headquarters and military staff. The Americans first military commander was a scholar named Robert Merriman, an assistant instructor of economics trained at the University of California at

---

book of poetry, in 1936, the same year he married Mary Wolfe. A few months later the Spanish Civil War began. After the Comintern began organizing international volunteers to help defend the Spanish Republic, Rolfe joined the International Brigades in the spring of 1937. Once in Spain he was assigned to edit the Volunteer for Liberty, the English-language magazine of the volunteers, in Madrid until joining the troops in the field in the spring of 1938. Rolfe's wife Mary joined him in Barcelona that fall. In January of 1939, the Rolfe's returned to the United States where the Spanish cause was already under attack. Martin Dies began congressional hearings on Communist activity and the volunteers who fought in Spain, as well as their supporters, were immediate suspects. Rolfe's brother Bern Fishman, a federal employee who had raised money for the fledgling Spanish republic came under scrutiny and Milt Wolff was called to testify before the House UnAmerican Activities Committee. While government harassment of the Lincoln Brigade veterans commenced, Random House published Rolfe's, The Lincoln Battalion, in 1939. He subsequently worked for the Soviet news agency TASS until he was drafted in 1943. Mary moved to Los Angeles and Rolfe joined her after the war where he published a mystery novel (The Glass Room) and found occasional work on the fringes of the film industry. He was blacklisted by the House Un-American Activities Committee in 1947 and continued to be active in the struggle against McCarthyism until his death, by heart attack, in 1954. Rolfe accrued the images in this collection in the course of his work as a journalist for the *Volunteer for Liberty* and the *Daily Worker*. Bio courtesy of Tamiment Library, NYU.

Berkeley, who had spent time researching economics in Russia before volunteering to fight fascism. Before he was a scholar, he was a field and industrial worker, and also worked in a paper mill, in log camps, in the Ford assembly plant, and in odd jobs such as a cement work. He led the Lincolns from their first days of battle until he was captured and executed, along with Dave Doran, the Lincoln political commissar, during the 1938 Spring Retreats at Gandesa.[37]

Americans in Battle

The American volunteers were trained to be a small assault force used on especially dangerous missions. Their first battle after training camp was in the Jarama Valley, southeast of Madrid. They engaged in trench warfare for four consecutive months – all the way from frigid February through the sweltering heat of June, 1937. The Republicans lost 25,000 fighters, including some of the best British and American members of the XVth Brigade. In one charge from their trenches on February 27, 1937, one-hundred and twenty-seven Americans died and nearly two hundred others were wounded. Only eighty men managed to navigate the battle physically unscathed.[38]

More than once, after that first attack on the Jarama Front, the Americans, believing their leadership had taken unnecessary risks with their lives, were on the

---

[37] John Tisa, *Recalling the Good Fight: An Autobiography of the Spanish Civil War* (South Hadley, Mass.: Bergin & Garvey Publishers, Inc., 1985) 53.

[38] Victor Hoar, "In Our Time: The Abraham Lincoln Brigade and the Historians" *American Quarterly*, Vol. 22, No. 1 (Spring, 1970), pp. 112-119.

verge of mutiny. Some deserted. A few were executed for being too afraid to leave the trenches. In July the Lincolns were sent northeast of Jarama to Brunete. The Washington Battalion was so decimated by Nationalist forces at Brunete that it was merged with the Lincolns prior to the Aragon Offensive, which took place from August to October, 1937. American International Brigaders stormed and captured the fortified strategic citadel towns of Quinto and Belchite, fighting at close range in the streets, throwing grenades and glycerin bottles into homes vacated by the civilian population, but occupied by Nationalist forces.

From December, 1937 to February, 1938 the English-speaking battalions fought for control of Teruel, southeast of Madrid. During the Retreats from March to April, 1938, Republican Forces, including the Lincolns, were outflanked by enemy tanks, strafed and bombed by huge fleets of Fiats, Messerschmitt, Junkers and Savoia-Marchettis, pounded by light and heavy artillery, and struggled to safety by swimming the swift-flowing, muddy Ebro River. Fewer than 100-150 Americans, who had already been decimated in earlier battles, survived the Retreats. Their last stand in Spain was the Ebro Offensive, which lasted from July to September 24, 1938. The men fought as a shock battalion, which helped stop the insurgent offensive against Valencia and kept enemy troops tied up for four months.[39]

Although each battle was its own, unique kind of hell-on-earth for the volunteers, there are broad patterns of continuity in each: The XVth waged surprise

---

[39] Edwin Wolfe, *The Lincoln Battalion* (New York, Random House, 1939).

attacks in a sector lightly manned by Nationalist forces; there was usually a break through enemy lines, followed by a rapid advance through enemy territory; prisoners were often taken, sometimes whole units that surrendered after shooting their officers; there was often a failure to capture some strategic strongpoint – usually a fortified town such as Quinto and Belchite – or a dominating height such as Mosquito Ridge; there was very often confusion and delays resulting from poor planning by leadership, coupled with scant resources and provisions, which gave Nationalist forces time to assemble troops for defense; most battles concluded with a Nationalist counteroffensive with overwhelming manpower and firepower, and a Loyalist retreat following bitter fighting against fascist forces who had superior numbers and firepower.[40]

By October, 1938, nine hundred of the twenty-eight hundred -- more than twenty-five percent – of American volunteers were buried in the Spanish earth, prompting Ernest Hemingway to famously write that "no men entered earth more honorably than those who died in Spain… They are immortal."[41] Concomitant to

---

[40] Malcolm Cowley, "Lament for the Abraham Lincoln Battalion," *The Sewanee Review*, Vol. 92, No. 3 (Summer, 1984), pp. 331-347.

[41] Hank Rubin, foreword by Peter N. Carroll, *Spain's Cause Was Mine: A Memoir of an American Medic in the Spanish Civil War* (Carbondale, Southern Illinois University Press, 1997) 153. Rubin was born May 21, 1916 in Portland, Oregon. He earned a BS from the University of California, Berkeley, member of the YCL. He sailed for Spain aboard the *Queen Mary* on July 7, 1937 and arrived July 20. He returned to the U.S. December 15, 1938. He lived in Los Angeles and worked as a bacteriologist.

the Brigades leaving Spain, Italy and Germany sent more men and more supplies to aid Franco's rebels. October, 1938 was the beginning-of-the-end of the Spanish War, and the official end for the American volunteers in Spain.

October, 1939, the same month Neville Chamberlain surrendered Czechoslovakia in the hope of preventing another World War, the American volunteers and the rest of the International Brigades were honored with a send-off parade in Barcelona. Dolores Ibarruri, "La Pasionaria" (The Passion Flower), who was considered one of the most vocal firebrands of the Republic's cause, told the volunteers that they had served "the cause of all advanced and progressive mankind." Many volunteers, especially those from Italy and Germany who had no homeland to return to, openly wept. She tried to comfort them by saying, "You can go proudly... You are history. You are legend."[42] But such platitudes provided no safe haven and little solace to the defeated.

Before leaving Barcelona in October, 1938, the surviving American volunteers who were not in Nationalist prison camps made a three-point pledge: 1. To continue to aid the Spanish people in their struggle against dictatorship in any way they could. 2. To acquaint Americans with the nature and danger of

---

[42] Ibarruri lived in Russia 36 years, until Franco's death, November 20, 1975. But the Soviets provided almost no sanctuary to the German and Italian volunteers who fought to defend the Spanish Republic. Many of them died in concentration camps. Don Lawson, *The Abraham Lincoln Brigade: Americans Fighting Fascism in the Spanish Civil War* (New York, Thomas Y. Crowell, 1989) 135.

fascism at home and abroad. 3. To aid fellow volunteers, care for the wounded and sick, and seek jobs for those able to work.[43] Ninety percent of the veterans also desperately needed jobs, seventy percent also needed some form of medical attention, and five percent were totally disabled beyond rehabilitation.[44] There was no severance pay other than a greyhound ticket and $25 for food along the way.[45] Many also surely suffered from post-traumatic stress disorder, although PTSD would not become a DSM diagnosis until many years after World War II.

When Spanish War officially ended in April, 1939, there were one hundred and four Americans survivors still in Nationalist prison camps. The eldest among them was Louis Ornitz, aged 27, the only survivor among the Americans taken near Brunete. His release, like that of the other prisoners, was delayed by quibbles within the State Department.[46] But between ninety and one hundred American volunteers were repatriated in April, 1939; a half dozen others were finally released in late August, 1939; the last four or five

---

[43] Arthur H. Landis, *The Abraham Lincoln Brigade* (New York, Citadel Press, 1967) 598.

[44] Cecil Eby, B*etween the Bullet and the Lie: American Volunteers in the Spanish Civil War,* (San Francisco, Holt, Rhinehart and Winston, 1969) 310.

[45] Hank Rubin, foreword by Peter N. Carroll, *Spain's Cause Was Mine: A Memoir of an American Medic in the Spanish Civil War* (Carbondale, Southern Illinois University Press, 1997) 153.

[46] Malcolm Cowley, "Lament for the Abraham Lincoln Battalion," *The Sewanee Review*, Vol. 92, No. 3 (Summer, 1984), pp. 331-347.

detained were not released for another full year, and were finally released in April 1940.[47] At the dock in New York their passports were seized. Though an enthusiastic crowd had gathered to welcome them home, it was forced back by police. After getting back to the States, many American volunteers were victims of the fascistic red hunters on the Dies Committee.

The End of Combat in Spain and the Start of a New War

By September, 1938, German and Italian manpower and firepower, together with a quasi-civil war between Communists and Anarchists inside Spain, and the persistent intercession of western democracies, had permitted Franco's forces to cut the Republic in two. Loyalist forces were on the run and backed into Catalonia. Any Spanish leaders with enough resources and sense began to see the end was in sight and had fled, including Juan Negrín y López, the Republic's head of state who was in exile in France. While pockets of resistance were especially recalcitrant in Catalonia and Aragon, the writing was on the wall for the Spanish Second Republic.

The withdrawal of the International Brigades effectively helped seal victory for Franco's rebels. The Republican government of Juan Negrín, who was backed by the Soviet Union, announced the decision in the League of Nations on September 21,1938, in Geneva, Switzerland. October, 1938, at the height of the Battle of the Ebro, the Non-Intervention Committee ordered the withdrawal of the International Brigades. The

---

[47] Arthur H. Landis, *The Abraham Lincoln Brigade* (New York, Citadel Press, 1967) 597

disbandment was part of an ill-advised effort to get the Nationalists' foreign backers – Italy and Germany -- to withdraw their troops and to persuade the western democracies such as France and Britain to end their arms embargo. The gamble did not pay off for anyone but the Fascists.[48]

On April 1, 1939, just two weeks after Hitler assumed control of Czechoslovakia, Franco declared total victory. August 23, 1939, Hitler and Stalin pragmatically signed a non-aggression pact. Seven months after the Republic of Spain fell to fascism, Hitler invaded Poland, thus officially beginning World War II; within five weeks, Hitler and Stalin were dividing Poland. The nations that had previously felt it in their best interest to leave the Spaniards to their own devices were soon forced to declare war on the Axis powers. On June 22, 1941, Hitler reneged on his non-aggression pact with Stalin and declared war on the Soviet Union. Four months later Japan bombed Pearl Harbor, ultimately pulling the U.S. out of isolation and ultimately to the center of geopolitics.

The American Volunteers After Spain

Despite the fact that the American volunteers were not fighting for communism or Bolshevism as many conservative critics declared, and despite the fact that the U.S. was allies with the Soviet Union during World War II, the state department considered very many American volunteers that went to aid the Second Spanish Republic to be security risks. In fact, FBI

---

[48] Hugh Thomas, *The Spanish Civil War* (New York, Random House, 2001) 683.

Director J. Edgar Hoover requested that President Franklin D. Roosevelt ensure that former International Brigade volunteers fighting in U.S. Forces during World War II not be considered for commissioning as officers, nor have any type of positive distinction conferred upon them.[49]

During World War II, many Lincoln vets, including Evelyn Hutchins, who was a truck driver in Spain, were used by the Rockefeller foundation and Yale University in preparing an Army survey to decipher the nature of fear and courage in industrialized combat. After the study was concluded, American vets of the Spanish War were deemed to be "pre-mature anti-fascists."[50] Despite often being treated as anti-American subversives due to their involvement in Spain, many American volunteers for Spain still loved their country and hated the threat of fascism to liberty, equality and fraternity at home and abroad. Although many believed there was a deep strain of fascism within their own government, and popular culture, many considered the Fascistic elements in the U.S. to be a less aggressive and therefore less evil version than the overt fascism propagated by the Axis Powers.

American volunteers for Spain, as such, volunteered again for the war they fought to prevent in the first place. Nearly half of those who fought to prevent World War II in Spain were casualties and nearly nine hundred died before Japan ever bombed Pearl Harbor. Four hundred more American volunteers

---

[49] Arthur H. Landis, *The Abraham Lincoln Brigade* (New York, Citadel Press, 1967) 169–173.

[50] Ibid, 599.

for the Spanish War were casualties, in Asian and European theaters of war.[51] Another twenty-five of them died in World War II.[52] The Lincolns who joined the U.S. Armed Forces during World War II were officially deemed "Suspected of Disloyalty" due to their involvement in Spain. And yet some five hundred Lincolns served in the Army. Most of them enlisted after Pearl Harbor without waiting to be drafted. Another three hundred joined the Merchant Marines. As regards the Lincolns in uniform, the Army never adopted a fixed policy; they were treated in various fashions at the whim of intelligence officers. Some of them were assigned to labor companies or to permanent KP duty. Some, such as Milt Wolff, served with Wild Bill Donovan in the Office of Strategic Services, which later became the Central Intelligence Agency.[53] Most of the Lincolns, however, distinguished themselves on the battlefield. Hermann Bottcher and Robert Thompson, for instance, earned Distinguished Service Crosses. Thompson swam a river under Japanese fire while towing a rope to which his men could cling before helping to wipe out two machinegun nests. His heroics against the Japanese, however, did not help him dodge the Cold War purge of leftists in the U.S. and he was convicted under the Smith

---

[51] Ibid, xix.

[52] Hank Rubin, foreword by Peter N. Carroll, *Spain's Cause Was Mine: A Memoir of an American Medic in the Spanish Civil War* (Carbondale, Southern Illinois University Press, 1997) 153.

[53] Cecil Eby, *Between the Bullet and the Lie: American Volunteers in the Spanish Civil War*, (San Francisco, Holt, Rhinehart and Winston, 1969) 315.

Act for allegedly advocating the overthrow of the government.[54]

What is perhaps one of the saddest ironies resulting from the war in Spain, World War II, and the Cold War is that, although many American volunteers went to Spain to stop fascism from spreading to the U.S., many of the volunteers, such as Thompson, were victims of fascism back home after surviving Franco, Hitler and Mussolini's forces. Things took an especially dark turn for many of them during the McCarthy Era, when the FBI and other governmental organizations and committees interpreted military service in Spain as loyalty to Stalin and the Soviet Union. In 1953, under the McCarran Act, which required registration of Communist Front organizations, the Attorney General filed a petition with the subversive Activities control board for an order requiring the VALB to register.[55] In 1955, the Subversive Activities Control Board declared that the organization was a front for the Communist

---

[54] The Smith Act was also known as The Alien Registration Act of 1940. It was enacted June 29, 1940, and set criminal penalties for advocating the overthrow of the U.S. government and required all non-citizen adult residents to register with the government. Approximately 215 people, including Thompson, were indicted under the legislation, including alleged communists, Anarchists, and fascists. Prosecutions under the Smith Act continued until a series of United States Supreme Court decisions in 1957 reversed a number of convictions under the Act as unconstitutional. See Malcolm Cowley, "Lament for the Abraham Lincoln Battalion," *The Sewanee Review*, Vol. 92, No. 3 (Summer, 1984), pp. 331-347.

[55] Cecil Eby, *Between the Bullet and the Lie: American Volunteers in the Spanish Civil War*, (San Francisco, Holt, Rhinehart and Winston, 1969) 315.

Party, although many members were not actually communists.[56]

By the 1960s Americans on the left were beginning to reassert themselves and more courageously critique the Cold War purges of liberals. On April 26, 1965, the Supreme Court finally vacated orders requiring registration of the VALB as a Communist front organization on the grounds that evidence was "too stale."[57] Besides, by 1967, less than five percent of American volunteers for the Spanish Republic had any affiliation (at least publicly) with Communist organizations, which especially speaks to the inherent infallibility of judging people's morality based on something as fluid as political persuasions can be.[58]

---

[56] Malcolm Cowley, "Lament for the Abraham Lincoln Battalion," *The Sewanee Review*, Vol. 92, No. 3 (Summer, 1984), pp. 331-347.

[57] Cecil Eby, *Between the Bullet and the Lie: American Volunteers in the Spanish Civil War*, (San Francisco, Holt, Rhinehart and Winston, 1969) 317.

[58] Landis, *The Abraham Lincoln Brigade* (New York, Citadel Press, 1967) 601.

Introduction

F. Jay Taylor wrote *The United States and the Spanish Civil War* in 1956, not long after the United States had assumed the mantle as the world's premier superpower. He called the Spanish War a "dress rehearsal" for World War II. Excepting the Great Depression and the hostilities that began in September, 1939, Jay wrote, "no public event of the 1930s mattered so much to so many Americans as did the Spanish Civil War.[59]

But what Jay and many other scholars erroneously refer to as the Spanish "Civil War" and as the "opening of World War II," and what Carlton Hayes, a former historian and U.S. ambassador to Spain, referred to as the "beginning of the Cold War," have overlooked the fact that the political discourse of the war in Spain from 1936 to 1939 was as much a continuation of the American, French, and Russian Revolutions as it was the beginning of World War II and/or Cold War.

Although scholars such as Allen Guttmann, Arthur Landis, Eric Hobsbawm, Taylor, and others have noted in passing the notion that fascism was the antithesis of the Enlightenment and also a kind of evolution of monarchy as a result of industrialization, and while others had noted that many American volunteers believed themselves to be fighting for values associated with the Enlightenment, nobody until now had really examined the American volunteers'

---

[59] F. Jay Taylor, *The United States and the Spanish Civil War* (New York, Bookman, 1956) 7.

correspondence to friends and family through the lens of Enlightenment era themes, tropes, and language.

As much as this project has been informed and inspired by the work of Guttmann, Landis, Hobsbawm and Taylor, it is equally informed by Chandra Manning's *What This Cruel War Was Over,* and also Wim Kloosters's *Revolutions in the Atlantic World: A Comparative History.*[60] Kloosters traces the Enlightenment era ideas and language that fueled some of the most seminal revolutionary movements in world history. Manning's study examines letters written by Union and Confederate soldiers during the American Civil War to find that most soldiers on both sides believed themselves to be fighting over the issue of slavery.

Fighting for the Enlightenment, similarly, focuses on wartime correspondence written by American soldiers who volunteered to defend the democratically elected Popular Front government against fascism in the Spanish War. One of the central themes and contributions of the study that follows is the elaboration

---

[60] Kloosters focuses on revolutions in British North America (1775-1783), France (1789-99), St. Dominique (1791-1804), and Spanish America (1810-24). The book compares these revolutions and shows how they were all intricately related. She, unlike R.R. Palmer, puts Haiti at the center of the story. The objective of the book is to present the most significant revolutions of the era on their own terms, emphasizing four aspects: 1. They can't be understood outside the realm of international politics. 2. None of the revolutions was foreordained. 3. Divided loyalties often meant that these wars were more like civil wars, whose main protagonists were previously voiceless popular classes fighting for their own reasons, which often did not jive with those of elites. 4. Democracy is no appropriate prism through which to understand these uprisings.

that the Spanish War was as much another chapter in the longue durée of revolutions inspired, in part, by Enlightenment era discourse, as much, if not more than, it was the opening stages of World War II and/or the beginning of the Cold War.

    This intellectual history, unlike most studies that focus on American volunteers, largely ignores battles and/or whether the Americans were heroic or not. Focusing on whether or not the American volunteers exhibited valor or heroism in battle would inevitably ensnare this project in the same Cold War-Culture War dialectic that much of the other scholarship produced by Spanish War vets and their critics, such as Cecil Eby, engaged in. Now that the Cold War has passed it is important to reassess the meanings and merits of the American volunteers' reasons for risking life, limb, and citizenship to fight Francisco Franco, Adolf Hitler and Benito Mussolini's Fascist forces in Spain.

    Despite the United States government's isolationism policy throughout the war in Spain, President Franklin Roosevelt gave adherents of the Spanish Republic a scintilla of hope in his October 1937 "Quarantine Speech;" he alluded to fascism as a disease that must be addressed, lest it spread throughout the world.[61] John Gates, formerly of City College of New

---

    [61] The following is an excerpt of Roosevelt's "Quarantine Speech": It is true that the moral consciousness of the world must recognize the importance of removing injustices and well-founded grievances; but at the same time it must be aroused to the cardinal necessity of honoring sanctity of treaties, of respecting the rights and liberties of others, and of putting an end to acts of international aggression. It seems to be unfortunately true that the epidemic of world lawlessness is spreading. When an epidemic of physical disease starts to spread, the community approves and joins in a quarantine of

York, who had risen to the rank of Commissar of war for XVth International Brigade wrote the following to President Roosevelt after the speech:

> Your speech showing way to democracies to oppose fascist aggressors who threaten to engulf the entire world in war to utter destruction of civilization fills us all with inspiration. The American, Canadian, and British volunteers of XV International Brigade together with their Spanish brothers are now in the frontline trenches defending counter-attack after counter-attack and defending with their lives the same ideals, same human values, same principles of individual freedom and democracy for the defense of which you raised your timely warning... To save Spain is to save democracy and peace throughout the world. Your high ideals, your statesmanship stand out in these dark hours of history as the showing of hope to all civilization. History, however, takes little

---

the patients in order to protect the health of the community against the spread of the disease. It is my determination to pursue a policy of peace and to adopt every practicable measure to avoid involvement in war. It ought to be inconceivable that in this modern era, and in the face of experience, any nation could be so foolish and ruthless as to run the risk of plunging the whole world into war by invading and violating, in contravention of solemn treaties, the territory of other nations that have done them no real harm and which are too weak to protect themselves adequately. Yet the peace of the world and the welfare and security of every nation is today being threatened by that very thing... War is a contagion, whether it be declared or undeclared.

account of good intensions; its monuments are built of deeds.[62]

Gates's letter, if nothing else, helps demonstrate the centrality of idealism to American volunteers' service to the Spanish Second Republic. But the Cold War-Culture Wars, which were especially fostered by New Deal liberalism, helped obscure the historical memory of why American volunteers decided to fight Franco, Hitler and Mussolini's fascist forces in the first place – which seems at least as important as how they got there and how they fared while in Spain. *Fighting for the Enlightenment*, as such, conscientiously focuses acutely on the reasons the nearly three thousand American volunteers believed they were in Spain while they were there by examining their correspondence to friends and family back home in the U.S.

Although each of the Americans who joined the International Brigades in defense of Spain's democratically elected government during Franco's two-and-half year military coup were incredibly unique, there are commonalities in the volunteers' correspondence. Themes especially prominent include Enlightenment era discourse – namely liberty, equality and fraternity. The discourse of liberty is particularly evident in volunteers' demands for freedom of religion, separation of church and state, and freedom of expression and speech. Equality is made especially manifest in volunteers' desire for a greater degree of

---

[62] Letter from John Gates, Commisar of war for XV International Brigade to President Roosevelt. Box 3, folder 38, Tamiment Library/Robert F. Wagner Labor Archives. Elmer Holmes Tamiment Library, 70 Washington Square South, New York NY 10012, New York University Libraries.

political and economic balance between social classes and races. Many American volunteers also often expressed a desire to see a classless society with greater racial equality. The language of equality is, of course, intricately connected to a discourse hailing fraternity for Spanish Republicans and especially for the United States.

Chapter One

"Psychology, Ideology, Idealism, and

The Will to Fight Fascism in the Great Depression"

Reasons for going to Spain were often as personal as they were idealistic. Some volunteers sought to restore their sense of masculinity in an age when the Great Depression had helped emasculate millions of men. "Going to war seemed for me a step into manhood," Hank Rubin wrote in his memoir. "I must confess that the imagery of personal heroism that accompanies soldiers in wartime appealed to me very much. It would be a heroic gesture that would be almost as good as composing a great symphony, painting a masterpiece, or writing the great American novel."[63]

John Cookson, a young scientist from Madison, Wisconsin, likewise noted the psychological component of wanting to go to Spain in a letter to his father: "Ever since mother's death," he wrote, "I find I don't have the fear of it (dying) which I had before."[64] Barney Bailey explained to himself his reasons for going to Spain in his diary from a trench outside Madrid when he wrote, "there's my self-respect to consider. If I failed to do my bit at a time like this, I'd never feel right afterward... I

---

[63] Hank Rubin, foreword by Peter N. Carroll, *Spain's Cause Was Mine: A Memoir of an American Medic in the Spanish Civil War* (Carbondale, Southern Illinois University Press, 1997) 12.

[64] John Cookson, June 27, 1937, in Cary Nelson and Jefferson Hicks, eds. *Madrid 1937: Letters of the Abraham Lincoln Brigade From the Spanish Civil War* (New York, Routledge, 1996) 36.

was born a rebel, a champion of the underdog... May I die that way when my time comes."[65] Comrades and roommates Jimmy Yates, Alonzo Watson, and Herman Wolfowitz made the decision to go to Spain after a long and heated late-night discussion in their Twelfth Street Loft in lower Manhattan. Bill Bailey went after feeling guilty as a result of receiving letters from seamen already in Spain. Truck driver, Evelyn Hutchins, likewise followed close friends, her brother, and her husband. Her sense of guilt, she said, was "alleviated only after she left for the war."[66]

For many American volunteers, Spain, in short, came to symbolize issues each was struggling with in their own personal lives. James Phillip Larder, for example, the son of Ring Lardner and a former Harvard student, wrote his mother a long letter from Barcelona, May 3, 1938, shortly before being killed in action, explaining the deeply personal motivations he had for risking his life in Spain:

> The decision has been very much my own, and I took it after a great deal of consideration. My closest friend and principal adviser here has been Vincent (Jimmy) Sheean, who told me not to join, which shows you how stubborn I am, if you didn't know. Ernest Hemingway's advice

---

[65] Peter Carroll, "Psychology & Ideology in the Spanish Civil War: The Case of the Abraham Lincoln Brigade" *The Antioch Review*, Vol. 52, No. 2, War (Spring, 1994), pp. 219-230.

[66] Hutchins as quoted in Justin Byrne in Peter N. Carroll & James D. Fernandez, *Facing Fascism: New York & The Spanish Civil War* (New York, NYU Press, 2007) 81.

was that it was a very fine thing if I wanted to fight against fascism, but that it was a personal matter that could only be decided by me... I have made up a list of reasons why I am enlisting in the International Brigade, which is fairly accurate, as I did it for my own information...

Because I believe that fascism is wrong and must be exterminated, and that liberal democracy or more probably communism is right.

Because my joining the International Brigade might have an effect on the amendment of the Neutrality Act in the United States.

Because after the war is over, I shall be a more effective anti-fascist.

Because in my ambitious quest for knowledge in all fields, I cannot afford in this age to overlook war.

Because I shall come into contact with a lot of communists, who are very good company and from whom I expect to learn new things.

Because I am mentally lazy and should like to do some physical work for a change.

Because I need something remarkable in my background to make up for my unfortunate self-consciousness in social relations.

Because I am tired of working for the *Herald Tribune* in particular and newspapers in general.

Because I think it will be good for my soul.

Because there is a girl in Paris who will have to learn that my presence is not necessary to her existence.

Because I want to impress various people.

Because I hope to find material for some writing, probably a play.

Because I want to improve my Spanish as well as my French.

Because I want to know what it is like to be afraid of something and I want to see how other people react to danger.

Because there may be a chance to do some reading and I won't have to wear a necktie.

Because I should like once more to get in good physical condition…

I have also considered a few reasons why I should not join the army, such as that I might get seriously wounded or killed and that I shall cause you many weeks of worry. I am sorry for your sake that they are not enough to dissuade me. If it is any comfort to you at all, I still hate violence and cruelty and suffering and if I survive this war do not expect to take any dangerous part in the next.[67]

---

[67] James Phillip Lardner, May 3, 1938, Folder 5, Box 20, Tamiment Library/Robert F. Wagner Labor Archives. Elmer Holmes Tamiment Library, 70 Washington Square

South, New York NY 10012, New York University Libraries. Lardner was born on May 18, 1914 in Chicago, Illinois. Though he expressed Communist sympathies, he had no official party affiliation. He was the second of four sons born to Ringgold (Ring) Wilmer Lardner, journalist and humorist, and Ellis Abbott Lardner, a Smith College graduate from a prominent Michigan family. In 1919, the Lardner family moved East and James, with his brothers, was raised in the affluent enclaves of Greenwich, Connecticut and Great Neck, Long Island. The boys came of age in the rich literary milieu formed by the writers and journalists the senior Lardners counted among their friends, including F. Scott and Zelda Fitzgerald, Dorothy Parker, Heywood Broun, and H. L. Mencken. Lardner attended Andover and Harvard and, following his education, was hired as reporter for the New York Herald Tribune. According to his brother, Ring Lardner, Jr., James' early journalism experiences were a "monotonous round of funerals, banquets, strikes, accidents and minor crimes ..." After three years in New York City, Lardner transferred to the *Herald Tribune's* Paris bureau in 1938. While there he began writing articles on the participation of American volunteers in the Spanish Civil War. In March 1938 Lardner traveled to Barcelona in the company of fellow journalists Ernest Hemingway and Vincent Sheean to observe the conflict first hand. After witnessing an aerial battle that destroyed a bridge on the Ebro River and the dire state of the Loyalist forces, Lardner resolved to join the International Brigades. His initial attempt to enlist found him in a ragged battalion in Badalona far from the field of action. Eager to participate in the conflict he left Badalona, made his way to Mora-la-Nueva, and enlisted in the Third Company of the Abraham Lincoln Brigade early in May. In July he sustained shrapnel injuries during his first battle. After a month of hospitalization, he was returned to active duty in the Sierra Pandols region near the Ebro. On September 23, 1938, on what was to be last day of fighting for the International Brigades, Lardner with two other men in his command were sent out to patrol a hill to the rear of his battalion. They encountered heavy enemy fire and Lardner did not return to camp. His death was confirmed several weeks later when a Nationalist correspondent reported that a body with foreign press credentials had been found in the location where Lardner was last seen. His body, which was discovered in fascist-controlled territory, was never recovered. According

Lardner's letter, though expressing an affinity towards communism as an anecdote to fascism, ultimately underscores how complexly personally volunteers' reasons could be for going to Spain.

But several decades of Cold War Culture Wars helped obscure the fact that Americans who went to Spain were not necessarily communists; and even those who were communists, were human beings whose thoughts and ideas had as much complexity, meaning, and value as Democrats and Republicans. Wilfred Mendelson's mother, who was, in fact, a member of the Communist Party, wrote the following to her son shortly after he went missing, never to be seen or heard from again:

> I started to write you several times in the past two weeks, but it seems so useless because we don't even know whether you'll ever read this or anything again... I would like to know what's happened to you... Dear son, just in case this reaches you just be assured that if modern medical science can do anything for you, it will be at your disposal regardless how much effort, money or anything else it takes... We always see you in our minds appearing or disappearing. Wilfred, I regret so bitterly that I was so long in joining the forces of progress, how much happier we would have been working together for the same things that are so dear to us instead of letting you do all the work and me all the

---

to Sheean, "Lardner, the last American to enlist, had been the last to be killed."

nagging... If only I could see you again... I love you and the things you taught me.[68]

Such heart-wrenching correspondence underscores the humanity and idealism of the volunteers willing to risk life, limb, and citizenship to defend the democratically elected government of the Republic of Spain against some of the same fascist forces the U.S. was forced to face a few years later in World War II. As such, the fact that thousands of Americans went to Spain or supported the Republic is testimony to their judgment and understanding of world events, and not necessarily to their politics or the ability of the Communist Party to dupe the American public.

Whether scholar, artist, poet, proletariat, or some combination thereof, many Americans volunteers' correspondence demonstrates devout idealism rooted in their psychological confrontation with the Great Depression.

Lack of faith in the nation and economic system (capitalism) during the 1930s stoked new critiques of the entire social system. Milt Felsen, for instance, remembered the 1930s as a time of great intellectual activity as a result of the economic and political turmoil:

> I went to Union Square and was amazed that there were speakers scattered throughout who

---

[68] Letter to Wilfred Mendelson from his mother, November 6, 1938, Brooklyn, New York. Box 6, Folder 15, Tamiment Library/Robert F. Wagner Labor Archives. Elmer Holmes Tamiment Library, 70 Washington Square South, New York NY 10012, New York University Libraries. Mendelson was one of many Jewish students from the City College of New York who volunteered for Spain.

stood on little boxes and could speak for hours about what was happening the world over without even pausing for breath. Everyone was reading like mad. Marx, Engels, Lenin, the *Daily Worker*, and books, tracts, and periodicals. Over a five-cent cup of coffee and the financial section of the *New York Times*, they would sit for hours tracing and analyzing the economic plunder being carried on by Wall Street's 'malefactors of great wealth. Most of the time I was unemployed and felt the devastating loss of self-worth that comes each day, watching the rest of the world get up and go someplace where they felt needed and useful... I felt I was a burden to myself and my family.[69]

Felsen's feelings of being a burden ultimately underscore the complex human emotions and psychological component of volunteers' decisions to risk life, limb and citizenship to go to Spain during the Great Depression. It also concomitantly illuminates the insidiousness of the Cold War-Culture Wars red baiting

---

[69] Milt Felsen, *The Anti-Warrior: A Memoir* (Iowa City, University of Iowa Press, 1989) 27-28. Born in New York City, *Milt Felsen* left the University of Iowa in his senior year to go to Spain in May of 1937. He served as a machine gunner in the Lincoln battalion and was wounded at Brunete. Upon release from the hospital, he spent the rest of the war as an ambulance driver. In World War Two, Felsen joined the Office of Strategic Services with other Lincoln veterans. Wounded and taken prisoner in North Africa, he spent two years in prisoner of war camps in Italy and Germany. Felson's memoir of childhood and the war years, *The Anti-Warrior*, was published by the University of Iowa in 1989. It is one of the few autobiographies by Lincoln veterans. It is a great read. Milt accomplished many things in peacetime. After the war, he worked for film-related labor unions in New York.

associated with conservatives' assailment of American volunteers' motives for going to Spain and concomitantly obscures the historical memory of the idealism in stark contrast to the cynicism associated with those who turned a blind eye to fascism in the 1930s.

"Don't worry about me," Canute Frankson, an African-American proletariat who volunteered to fight on behalf of the Spanish Republic, wrote a friend in 1937. "Even if I should be killed I'll die fighting for you, our people who suffer the bitter scourge of the lynch law, for the class to which I belong, and for the cause of freedom and democracy."[70] Ely Sack likewise wrote of the importance of his service in a letter to his parents; "it would make me very happy if I knew that in some way

---

[70] Canute Frankson to friend, Steve Nelson Box1, Folder, Canute Frankson Letters From Spain June 26, 1937. Tamiment Library/Robert F. Wagner Labor Archives. Elmer Holmes Tamiment Library, 70 Washington Square South, New York NY 10012, New York University Libraries. Frankson was born in the Parish of St. Catherine, Old Harbor, Jamaica on April 13, 1890. In 1917, together with his wife, Rachel, he emigrated to Wilkes Barre, Pennsylvania, where Frankson worked as a machinist. Frankson eventually settled in Detroit, where he worked in the auto industry. Frankson joined the Communist Party in 1934. He sailed for Europe aboard the Queen Mary on April 21, 1937. In Spain, skilled machinists were scarce and Frankson with his proven ability was rapidly promoted. He was appointed Head Mechanic at the International Garage in Albacete. Fellow International Garage veteran, Marion Noble, noted that Frankson's fluency in Spanish was a great asset and that many hours of his free time were spent teaching engine repair classes to young Spaniards. Frankson returned to the United States aboard the President Harding on September 24, 1938. Frankson was killed in an auto accident in either 1939 or 1940. Bio courtesy of Tamiment Library.

you too are helping the Spanish people," he wrote. "Because there is nothing more important."[71]

Many volunteers, such as New York University law student Leonard Levenson, viewed the war as an apocalyptic battleground between the revolutionary

---

[71] Ely Sack Papers, ALBA.094, Folder, Ely Sacks to his parents; June 27, 1937, SRI #137, Albacete Spain. Tamiment Library/Robert F. Wagner Labor Archives. Elmer Holmes Tamiment Library, 70 Washington Square South, New York NY 10012, New York University Libraries. Ely Joseph Sack was born September 19, 1915 in Brooklyn, New York to Russian Jewish immigrant parents. After graduating from New Utrecht High School in 1931, Sack worked at low-paying day jobs while attending night classes in accounting at the City College of New York School of Commerce. Sack left the United States aboard the M/V Georgic to England on May 15, 1937. From England he traveled through France and over the Pyrenees to Spain to fight for the Republican cause in the Spanish Civil War. Sack trained at Tarazona de la Mancha between June and September 1937. In September 1937 his unit of the MacKenzie-Papineau Battalion served a reserve unit, then went into combat at Fuentes del Ebro in October, 1937. Sack spent some time in Officer's Training School in November, 1937 but returned to fighting with his unit after about a month. In March, 1938 Sack was wounded in his left leg and was disabled for the remainder of his time in Spain. Sack was first treated in Tortosa then in Benacasim where he had an operation to remove shrapnel from his left leg and tetanus from his right leg. He spent time healing in Murcia. He was later moved to Mataro where his left leg was operated on twice more in May, 1938. Sack was discharged and repatriated in July, 1938. Sack returned to the United States via France on the S.S. De Grasse in August, 1938. Upon his return, Sack married Edith Berk, whom he had met in 1935. In 1939 the couple moved to Jacksonville, Florida where they raised five children while Sack worked as an accountant. In 1972 they moved to Miami, and they also lived for a short time in the early 1980s in Birmingham, Alabama. Sack continued to work in accounting well into his seventies. Biography courtesy of Tamiment Library, NYU.

working classes and the forces of fascist reaction. "I'm fighting for a cause which concerns the entire world," he wrote in earnest to his family. "It's not a dedication to abstract ideals either; it's a gruesome fight for all your lives and the future. What we're doing here is inextricably connected with your routine existence. Spain must be the sepulochre [sic] of Hitler and Mussolini. It must also be the first crushing blow against the system which has made our lives such a poignant struggle against odds."[72]

In short, correspondence written by many American volunteers indicate that they were – for good or ill, naïve or not – guided by a deep sense of idealism and altruism. "We are thoroughly convinced of the cause for which we fight," Frankson wrote a friend in 1937. "Our minds are made up for the sacrifices ahead. We fight with a zeal which can only be found in the hearts of men who represent an ideal."[73]

And as the threat of fascism in Europe grew, thousands of idealists, particularly artists, professionals, workers and students, found themselves drawn out of

---

[72] Leonard Levenson papers, ALBA.151, Box 1. Tamiment Library/Robert F. Wagner Labor Archives. Elmer Holmes Tamiment Library, 70 Washington Square South, New York NY 10012, New York University Libraries. He misspelled sepulture, which is defined as a burial or internment. He graduated from NYU and Georgetown Law. CCNY as an undergrad. He arrived in Spain June 20, 1937 aboard the *Britannic* and returned December 15, 1938 aboard the *Paris*.

[73] Canute Frankson to friend, Steve Nelson Papers, ALBA.008, Box 1, Folder: Canute Frankson Letters From Spain. Tamiment Library/Robert F. Wagner Labor Archives. Elmer Holmes Tamiment Library, 70 Washington Square South, New York NY 10012, New York University Libraries.

ordinary life and into extraordinary commitments on behalf of liberty, equality and fraternity. Gates, Sack, Frankson, Levenson, and many American volunteers' wartime correspondence help indicate that simplifying the reasons American volunteers risked life, limb and citizenship to reductionist and politically motivated Cold War-Culture War rhetoric such as they were "fighting for communism" or "against fascism" is far too abstract and thus obscures the complexity of the psyche and emotions of the nearly three thousand Americans who went to Spain.

After the Spanish War, researchers at Yale University, funded by the Rockefeller Foundation, who were determined to decipher the psychological reasons why people were willing to risk their lives in war asked Evelyn Hutchins – the only female involved in the study – why she was willing to risk her safety in a faraway land that was not her own. She especially stressed idealism in coping with danger. Many volunteers' initial decision to go to Spain had often involved a genuine psychological conversion resulting from social inequity, which they believed to be inherently wrong. Many of their motives were often rooted in their personal struggle with the Great Depression. Many felt they were struggling with the same forces and power structures in Spain that were synonymous with the forces many had battled along picket lines and wildcat strikes in the U.S. Many volunteers, therefore, reluctantly faced incredible terror, accepted discipline of their oft incompetent officers, and fought against overwhelming military superiority, due to, as their letters often evince, their commitment to Enlightenment Era principles such as liberty, equality and fraternity.[74]

In other words, many American volunteers did not go to Spain to defend communism or spread Bolshevism; they went for reasons that go much deeper and are far more personal than things as flimsy and fluid as political persuasions. Many American volunteers who went to Spain to fight to defend the Republic's democratically elected government went to confront the inherent inequity that was part and parcel of Depression-era capitalism, which helped, in part, usher in an era of unreasonable demagoguery and fascism in Europe and many other places throughout the world.

From 1936 to 1939 Spain became the focal point for many American volunteers' idealism. Robert Munson Taylor, for example, said as much to a friend from a trench in Spain, writing that "we are idealists fighting for something which we know is right in every degree."[75] In April 1937, Dartmouth graduate, Joe Dallet, along with dozens of other volunteers, crowded onto small fishing-boats and were arrested by French police in the Mediterranean en route to International Brigade headquarters in Albacete, Spain. During their hearing in front of a French court, their lawyer professed, "There are laws and laws, crimes and crimes. Theirs is a political crime – that they love liberty, democracy and

---

[74] Peter Carroll, "Psychology & Ideology in the Spanish Civil War: The Case of the Abraham Lincoln Brigade" *The Antioch Review*, Vol. 52, No. 2, War (Spring, 1994), pp. 219-230.

[75] Robert Munson Taylor, April 20, 1937, in Marcel Acier, ed, *From Spanish Trenches: Recent Letters From Spain* (New York, Modern Age, 1937) 151.

peace. Before this court I want to pay homage to these twenty-five Americans who left homes, jobs, and families and friends to fight for their ideals."[76] After Dallet was killed in action in Spain, his sister Peg wrote to her parents and siblings that, "I've always said Joe was the happiest of us all because he knew what he wanted to accomplish and unselfishly and without regard to his physical safety, he spent the last ten years of his life accomplishing what he could to further his ideals."[77]

---

[76] Joe Dallet, "Letters From Spain, American Volunteer to His Wife" (New York, Workers Library Publishers, 1938), 19. Dallet paraphrased his lawyer in a letter written to his wife. Box 2, folder 60, Tamiment Library/Robert F. Wagner Labor Archives. Elmer Holmes Tamiment Library, 70 Washington Square South, New York NY 10012, New York University Libraries.

[77] Joe Dallet Papers, ALBA.032, Box 1, folder: 1929-1937. Tamiment Library/Robert F. Wagner Labor Archives. Elmer Holmes Tamiment Library, 70 Washington Square South, New York NY 10012, New York University Libraries. Joseph Dallet, Jr. (1907-1937) was born into an affluent family in Woodmere, NY on Long Island. His parents, Joseph Sr. and Hilda, provided a childhood filled with cultural and educational opportunities and travel. Dallet attended the Woodmere Academy prior to high school, and eventually enrolled at Dartmouth University. He would have graduated in 1927, but became disillusioned with formal education and left. After working for a short time in the insurance business, he moved in 1928 to the Midwest and became involved with the labor movement. Repudiating his privileged background, he worked as a longshoreman in the late 1920s and in the steel mills of Pennsylvania and Ohio in the early 1930s. A militant labor organizer, he joined the Communist Party, U.S.A. in 1929. In the same year he married his first wife, Barbara Rand, who was also active in the labor movement; they would later divorce. During the next several years he lived in Pennsylvania and Ohio, where he became a member of the Communist Party of Ohio. Known as a political militant who affected a tough,

The scant pay, inferior firepower, and especially limited rations serve as evidence that many American volunteers were by no means mercenaries for the Soviet Union, as many conservative critics later claimed. "Most of us who went to Spain were politically conscious," Charles Hall, a former University of Chicago student wrote in his unpublished memoir. "The number who were mercenaries, high paid aviators (much featured in the press), adventurers seeking a thrill, were very few."[78]

---

pseudo-proletarian style, he became a well-known figure in working-class communities throughout the Midwest, organizing rallies, leading meetings and giving speeches. He ran for mayor of Youngstown, OH on the Communist ticket in 1935. In 1934 Dallet met and married his second wife, Katherine (Kitty) Peunig (later to become Mrs. J. Robert Oppenheimer). Dallet's interests eventually turned toward helping the Spanish Republic defeat General Franco and his fascist rebels. He signed on with the Abraham Lincoln Brigade in New York, and in March of 1937 sailed to Europe with plans to enter Spain via the French border. On March 27th, however, he and a group of volunteers were arrested just off the coast of Spain by French authorities. After serving twenty-one days in prison, Dallet tried again to make his way to Spain, succeeding on April 22nd by way of the Pyrenees. Because of his years of political and organizing experience, Dallet was appointed as a Commissar, with responsibilities for political indoctrination, education, and morale building, in the Mackenzie-Papineau Battalion, a unit comprised of both Canadian and U.S. volunteers. The Battalion was mustered into the International Brigade in July 1937. Dallet was sometimes resentful of the political assignment that kept him from front-line action, and his harsh, authoritarian leadership style drew criticism from the ranks. At last he got his chance, and on October 17, 1937, while leading his unit into battle on the Aragon Front, he was shot and killed. At the time of his death, Kitty was on her way to Paris in hopes of traveling to Spain to visit him, and to work in some capacity for the Loyalist cause. Biography courtesy of Tamiment Library, NYU.

[78] Charles Hall, "The Story of San Pedro and Spain" (unpublished memoir), Box 3, folder 116, Tamiment

John Cookson, a PhD candidate at the University of Wisconsin, wrote his Aunt Mabel the following spirited rebuttal from a Spanish trench after she insinuated that he was a mercenary for the Soviet Union:

> You say I should not waste my life – for money... A soldier gets (at the present exchange rate for the peseta) something like 18 cents a day and at the front 21 cents a day, and as an officer I get at the front some 75 cents a day and return 50 cents of this back to organizations for relief... Ever since you have pointed out the North star to me 22 years ago, I have followed it in the duel sense of the French way "Etoille" – star and destiny. The light of scientific truth can never be neglected by humans. I am absolutely certain of my convictions and you know now I have followed them in the face of death... England, the mighty British Empire reversing his stand, the American people reversing their stand, the greatest scientists, politicians, writers, artists, and statesmen calling for active help for Spain and many giving their work and life here...The whole thing cannot be properly understood unless we are capable of understanding the role fascism is playing in the modern world. Fascism is but a powerful organization of finance capital for thwarting the people and the working class in particular to achieve their own well-being at

---

Library/Robert F. Wagner Labor Archives. Elmer Holmes Tamiment Library, 70 Washington Square South, New York NY 10012, New York University Libraries. Born in South Dakota, moved to Chicago with his parents. He quit school during the Depression, went to Spain in 1937, and was a POW for 13 months.

the expense of a powerful minority...To defeat
fascism would ensure a final victory for the
forces of progressive and advanced humanity...
I submitted myself voluntarily, as have 3,000
other Americans, and surely not for 21 or 75
cents a day, nor for adventurism, nor for any
other hypothesis you may advance – they can be
but for one thing – to follow the bright star of
your beliefs to the bitter end, though it be death
itself. Remember, no one person is worth very
much in this world. There are tens of thousands
of young physicists that can do the work better
than ever I can. I do not see it as a waste of one's
life... I shall always work and fight for a society
where the initiative to work is not one of profit,
but one where the greatest good is done for the
greatest number.[79]

The spirit of Cookson's idealism – naïve or not – is more normative than exceptional in relation to other American volunteers' letters. The language of enlightened romanticism is uncannily common in their correspondence. Such idealism cost many of them, Cookson included, their lives.

The American volunteers' idealism was especially deduced by writer Joseph Beach, who was embedded with Republican forces: "Since the beginning of the Civil War in Spain," he wrote, "I have been for the

---

[79] John Cookson, October 2, 1937, Albacete, Spain, in Cary Nelson and Jefferson Hicks, eds. *Madrid 1937: Letters of the Abraham Lincoln Brigade From the Spanish Civil War* (New York, Routledge, 1996) 37-38. He sailed aboard the *Champlain* January 23, 1937 and was killed in action September 12, 1938 – just weeks before the International Brigades were sent home.

loyalist government, because it represents republican and representative institutions as opposed to arbitrary and dictatorial rule, because it represents the economic and cultural interests of the great body of the population, and because it gives the greatest hope for a modern and effective organization of society."[80] American volunteer, Eugene Wolman, likewise summarized the idealism of fighting in Spain when he wrote to his father, "I seem selfish, but if you consider what I am doing it will appear at least an enlightened selfishness."[81] The volunteers were, by any calculable measure, asked to take terrible risks and perform impossible feats. Only a deep sense of commitment to a cause of great importance – an enlightened selfishness -- made such a sacrifice and gamble possible.[82] The Americans, as Malcolm Cowley said, "can never be deprived of that original, pristine conviction that a man ought to be willing to give himself for an ideal."[83]

But as much as the Great Depression shaped and molded volunteers' idealism and psychology, the

---

[80] Joseph Beach, *Writers Take Sides* (New York, 1938) 4.

[81] Eugene Wolman, March 13, 1938 in Cary Nelson and Jefferson Hicks, eds. *Madrid 1937: Letters of the Abraham Lincoln Brigade From the Spanish Civil War* (New York, Routledge, 1996) 30-31. Born January 4, 1913 in New York City. Sailed aboard the *Aquitania* March 31, 1937; Killed in Action, July 1937 in Brunete.

[82] Cary Nelson and Jefferson Hicks, eds. *Madrid 1937: Letters of the Abraham Lincoln Brigade From the Spanish Civil War* (New York, Routledge, 1996) 308.

[83] Malcolm Cowley, "Lament for the Abraham Lincoln Battalion," *The Sewanee Review*, Vol. 92, No. 3 (Summer, 1984), pp. 331-347.

1930s did not happen in a vacuum. Many volunteers were scholars and even many of those who were not academics seemed acutely aware that the power relations associated with fascism was relational to monarchy and the series of revolutions and counter-revolutions that had fueled history from the Age of Revolutions in the eighteenth and nineteenth century all the way through the Bolshevik Revolution and the 1930s.[84]

Thusly, however much they might attempt to stifle their private egos as their commanding officers wished and instructed them to do, each American volunteer, as the study at Yale deduced, was an individual that perceived themselves to be "daring, audacious," and part of the "vanguard of human history."[85]

---

[84] The Enlightenment is the period in the history of western thought and culture, stretching roughly from the mid-decades of the seventeenth century through the eighteenth century, characterized by dramatic revolutions in science, philosophy, society and politics. Enlightenment thought *culminates* historically in the political upheaval of the French Revolution, in which the traditional hierarchical political and social orders (the French monarchy, the privileges of the French nobility, the political power and authority of the Catholic Church) were violently destroyed and replaced by a political and social order informed by the Enlightenment ideals of freedom and equality for all, founded, ostensibly, upon principles of human reason.

[85] Peter Carroll, "Psychology & Ideology in the Spanish Civil War: The Case of the Abraham Lincoln Brigade" *The Antioch Review*, Vol. 52, No. 2, War (Spring, 1994), pp. 219-230. Carroll is not himself making this statement, but evoking Dr. Pike's finding in his study on the psychological and

Chapter Two

"Scholars, Artists and Idealists"

Eric Hobsbawm wrote in 2007 that the Spanish Civil War was a war of intellectuals, poets, writers and artists who flocked to the anti-fascist cause, only to be badly let down by the workers and peasants of Europe, who refused to respond to the appeal of the left. But neither assessment is a completely apt way of describing the American volunteers. Though they were heavily represented by artists and intellectuals, including Brooklyn College English professor David McKelvy White, whose father was a former governor of Ohio, most of the Americans were, in fact, so-called workers and peasants of European ancestry -- including seamen, manual workers, longshoremen, truck drivers, and mechanics. Proletariats were far more common amongst the American volunteers than the more famous writers, painters, poets, and other educated volunteers who were, admittedly, far more self-consciously active in documenting their experiences in letters and memoirs than the workers tended to be.

More than seventy nationalities were also represented in the ranks of the American battalions. The vast majority of American volunteers, whether workers, artists and/or intellectuals, were products of the immigrant generation – Irish, Jews, Italians, Slavs, and Greeks – whose parents had escaped persecution and poverty in European cities and hinterlands for the hope of better lives in the United States.

---

ideological imperatives inspiring the Lincolns to volunteer to go to Spain.

Unemployment, poverty, the interruption of education, careers, and relationships, which were part and parcel of the Great Depression, helped to make volunteers especially sympathetic and receptive to the socially progressive goals of the Spanish Second Republic.[86] The glue that held the scholars, artists and workers in the American battalion together – despite their ethnic and socioeconomic differences – was the egregious affront to the values associated with the Enlightenment that fascism represented during the Great Depression.[87]

In other words, a careful examination of American volunteers' wartime correspondence helps demonstrate that despite the myriad socioeconomic and regional differences in their backgrounds, most volunteers' letters indicate that a high percentage of them genuinely believed they were fighting for values associated with Enlightenment era discourse, namely

---

[86] Fraser Ottanelli in Peter N. Carroll & James D. Fernadez, *Facing Fascism: New York & The Spanish Civil War* (New York, NYU Press, 2007) 63; and also Peter N. Carroll, *The Odyssey of the Abraham Lincoln Brigade: Americans in the Spanish Civil War* (Stanford, CA: Stanford University Press, 1994) 74.

[87] Tim Buch, the General Secretary of CP Canada alluded to the bond after Dallet's death. His death in action with our Mackenzie-Papineau Battalion is one more seal in the sacred bond of international comradeship which binds together our fellow Canadians, Americans, Europeans, workers, poets, artists and soldiers in that proud Army of volunteers whose deeds have made their very own the deathless shout of embattled democracy: 'They shall not pass.'" Published in Joe Dallet, "Letters From Spain, American Volunteer to His Wife" (New York, Workers Library Publishers, 1938), 5. Dallet paraphrased his lawyer in a letter written to his wife. Box 2, folder 60, ALBA, Tamiment Library, NYU.

liberty, equality and fraternity. To many of the American volunteers Hitler, Mussolini and Franco represented feudalism, race hatred, abuse of power, class-based divisions of society, anti-progressivism, and, ultimately, the antithesis of liberty, equality and fraternity.

Many American scholars, artists, and proletariats who volunteered to fight fascism in Spain were especially cognizant of their emerging place in human history, most notably as part of the series of revolutions and counter-revolutions that had occurred since the eighteenth century, of which many perceived Spain to be another chapter in the long durée of the Age of Revolutions that Karl Marx had prophesied.

Perhaps none of the American volunteers for Spain were more cognizant of and invested in the notion of defending the principles of the Enlightenment than the scholars, such as John Cookson. **American colleges, especially in New York City and the Ivy League, were particularly active hubs of sympathy for the Spanish Republic. College students were the second largest group to volunteer, outnumbered only by seamen.**[88]

More than five hundred (one sixth of) volunteers came from campuses across the country and from virtually all fields of study. A number of them had excellent academic records, several were serious enough about school to be working on graduate degrees, and one soldier had his Phi Beta Kappa key delivered to him

---

[88] For an interesting examination of sailors and seamen being central to revolutions in the Atlantic World see Peter Linebaugh and Marcus Rediker's *The Many Headed Hydra: Sailors, Slaves, Commoners, and Hidden History of the Revolutionary Atlantic* Boston, Beacon Press, 2000).

in a Spanish trench.[89] The University of California at Berkeley was also very well represented amongst the ranks of American volunteers and it especially "generated brainpower that scanned and probed the serious problems of the world," Marion Merriman wrote in her memoir about her and her husband's time in Spain. "At Berkeley, Bob began to reach deeply into life itself, beyond himself, beyond the campus… Economics and its repercussions were natural preoccupations for Berkeley students, whose logic ran as cool as their passions ran hot."[90]

Jewish students were also apt to fight Hitler's insidious brand of fascism and race hatred. At least nineteen of the twenty-two volunteers from New York University were Jewish, as were no fewer than seventy-five percent of the sixty students, faculty and alumni from City College of New York, which was almost

---

[89] Robert A. Rosenstone, "The Men of the Abraham Lincoln Battalion," *The Journal of American History*, Vol. 54, No. 2 (Sep., 1967), pp. 327-338.

[90] Dr. Ira B. Cross taught them to find new ways to make the world better. He told them, this is your duty. There are solutions, but you must work hard to find them. The world must improve. Without you, it won't happen. It's that simple. You, the gifted ones with the brains and energy, you make the difference. See Marion Merriman and Warren Lerude, *American Commander in Spain: Robert Hale Merriman and the Abraham Lincoln Brigade* (Reno, University of Nevada Press, 1986) 17. Marion Merriman arrived in Albacete to unite with her wounded husband Robert. She joined the Lincoln Battalion, becoming the only female member, and worked on the Battalion newsletter, typed death certificates and re-typed much-needed training manuals with carbon paper for distribution to the men. James Anderson, *The Spanish Civil War: A History and Reference Guide* (Westport, CT, Greenwood Press, 2003) 138.

certainly the educational institution in the country with the largest number of volunteers represented in the American ranks of the International Brigades. CCNY had free tuition and an eighty percent Jewish student body – many of them were from the outer boroughs. Branded the "Little Red School House" by the popular press, CCNY was an especially active leftist political hub during the Great Depression, when students and faculty often partnered in initiatives to protest against the introduction of tuition fees, the student military training corps, and restrictions on freedom of speech imposed by the politically conservative college president Frederick B. Robinson. Campus politics dovetailed into broader issues at home and abroad, particularly opposition to imperialism, fascism and racism. Tension at City College peaked in October 1934 when twenty-one students, including a future volunteer, Wilfred Mendelson, were expelled for disrupting a meeting given by a delegation of Italian Young Fascists.[91]

Many of the college educated volunteers also expressed the belief that going to Spain was a logical extension of their classroom education. John Field, a track and cross-country star at the University of Rochester who graduated in 1935, wrote home from Spain to a friend to explain that his wartime experience equated to first-class "courses having to do with political economy, sociology, labor history, and philosophy." Ernest Amatniek, a scientist at CCNY, explained to a friend that, "Our job is to learn and experiment in this

---

[91] Justin Byrne in Peter N. Carroll & James D. Fernadez, *Facing Fascism: New York & The Spanish Civil War* (New York, NYU Press, 2007), 79.

science of killing the enemy before he kills us."[92] The following excerpt from a letter from John Cookson to his father especially demonstrates the conviction of the scholars who fought Franco's fascists:

> As you know we've spent many hours together in Madison talking about the next war... My university work and all the wonderful laboratory equipment which was available to me was the strongest attachment I had. Also, I stopped when near the final drive for my doctorate. Further, to come here, I knew meant possible loss of citizenship and least of all loss of my U.S. Army commission. But you also know that by conviction and action, theory and practice, I had turned "revolutionary" the past two years. The most revolutionary thing one can do now is to fight fascism. The truth of this I am now more certain than ever before. Hence, since I have tried to follow my life in accordance with dialectical materialism it was the only action I could take. No one spoke to me about it.[93]

But whether anyone actually talked to or recruited Cookson to abandon his studies for a warzone in Spain does not mean he was not, at least

---

[92] Ernest Amatniek, Box 1, Folder 21, ALBA, Tamiment Library, NYU. August 11, 1937, October 11, 1937, December 4, 1937. Albacete, Spain and Villa Rosa, Luxemburg. Born in Tallin, Estonia; came to the U.S. at age 14. Attended City College.

[93] John Cookson, June 27, 1937, Socorro Rojo Internacional, Albacete, Spain, in Cary Nelson and Jefferson Hicks, eds. *Madrid 1937: Letters of the Abraham Lincoln Brigade From the Spanish Civil War* (New York, Routledge, 1996) 35.

subconsciously, convinced to go by an array of creative productions designed to critique fascism in the 1930s. American creative writers – especially in New York and Hollywood – whether or not they accepted American neutrality, were overwhelmingly opposed to Franco, Hitler and Mussolini's forces. *Blockade,* which premiered in theaters in 1938, and featured a young Henry Fonda playing a Spanish peasant oppressed by Nationalists, for instance, explained to viewers that the rebellion was "not a war," but "murder" in an unbridled attempt to win popular support for the Republic amongst movie-going Americans.[94]

The short-lived Spanish Second Republic provided public support for artists, writers, and intellectuals in an outburst of constructive energy that thrilled their own people as well as progressives throughout the world.[95] Anti-fascist art was also prominent in American popular culture during the Great Depression and the era of the Popular Front. Many artists were particularly invested in fighting the threat of fascist expansion throughout the world via their art. Two art shows in New York City especially addressed themes connected to the war in Spain. The first, titled "To Aid Democracy in Spain," was held October 1936, and the second, "In Defense of World Democracy: Dedicated to the Peoples of Spain and

---

[94] William Dieterle, *Blockade* (1938).

[95] Milt Felsen, *The Anti-Warrior: A Memoir* (Iowa City, University of Iowa Press, 1989) 33.

China," took place in December 1937.[96] After returning to his studies at UCLA, following his service to the Republic of Spain as a medical professional, Hank Rubin arranged for an exhibit of contemporary (meaning wartime) Spanish art. The show featured paintings and ink sketches from the brush and pen of Sim (Rey Vila), a Catalonian artist, and José Bardasano, a painter from Basque, who depicted pictures of fascist cruelty and worker solidarity.[97]

Propaganda posters produced by artists such as Sim and Bardasano constituted one of the most poignant sources that survived the war in Spain because they provided an essential part of the visual landscape in which individuals living in the midst of that tragedy went about their daily business of survival. Robert Merriman, an American volunteer fighting in Spain, wrote from Barcelona in January of 1937 that the streets were "aflame with posters of all parties for all causes, some of them put out by combinations of parties."[98] Of

---

[96] Helen Langa in Peter N. Carroll & James D. Fernadez, *Facing Fascism: New York & The Spanish Civil War* (New York, NYU Press, 2007) 106.

[97] Hank Rubin, foreword by Peter N. Carroll, *Spain's Cause Was Mine: A Memoir of an American Medic in the Spanish Civil War* (Carbondale, Southern Illinois University Press, 1997) 155.

[98] Merriamn as quoted in "The Visual Front," Posters of the Spanish Civil War From UCSD's Southworth Collection: http://libraries.ucsd.edu/speccoll/visfront/intro. In Republican territory, when a house was destroyed by the enemy bombs, propaganda agencies would fix posters on the ruins in order to denounce the enemy, hoping to turn aggression into rage. In Madrid, the capital of the Republic, shop owners were exhorted to fill their store fronts with posters: An October 30, 1936, an article in the newspaper *ABC*

course, no single work of art was more synonymous with the Spanish War than Pablo Picasso's *Guernica*, which hung in New York's museum of Modern Art for many years during Franco's reign in Spain (1939 to 1975).[99] Paul Robeson also sang to wounded soldiers in the International Brigade hospital in Benicasim on the Mediterranean Sea. Errol Flynn also visited soldiers.[100] Both Woodie Guthrie and Pete Seeger's Almanac Singers made their New York debuts at fundraisers for Spanish refugee relief in 1940 and 1941; Lincoln Battalion ballads were recorded by Pete Seeger, Tom Glazer, and Bess and Baldwin Hawes in New York City in 1944 (and re-issued in 1961 and 1962). At the 1964 Newport Folk Festival, Phil Ochs joked that, "I wouldn't be surprised to see an album called 'Elvis Presley Sings Songs of the Spanish Civil War.'" Ochs wrote a song condemning American travelers for supporting Franco's regime with tourist dollars. What Bob Dylan had by 1964 criticized as the "politics of ancient history," were actually more timely than his lack of historical memory allowed him to perceive, considering the idealism and defiance associated with the American volunteers for Spain was

---

declared that "every space must be used to incite the spirit in its fight against the enemy."

[99] On April, 26, 1937 the German Condor Legion bombed the town of Guernica, killing 200-300 and causing significant damage to property. Pablo Picasso's *Guernica* (1937) took inspiration from the bombing of Guernica. *Guernica*, like many important Republican masterpieces, was featured at the 1937 International Exhibition in Paris.

[100] James Anderson, *The Spanish Civil War: A History and Reference Guide* (Westport, CT, Greenwood Press, 2003) 146.

"radical chic" by the end of the turbulent decade that helped fuel Dylan's stardom.[101]

But art was not just influencing volunteers' sense of idealism. Some of the men in the International Brigades were also creating cultural productions that influenced people back in the U.S.[102] Among Spanish Republicans, especially great value was placed on poetry, letters and essays. And no International Brigader anguished, perhaps, more about the tensions between political responsibility and creative individualism than the poet Edwin Rolfe, a member of the Lincoln Battalion, who wrote a poem about his experience in the war with the lamentation, "You remain, Madrid, the conscience of our lives."[103]

The American volunteers were an incredibly eclectic cadre of communitarian-minded individuals, including Greenwich Village painters like Douglas Taylor and Deyo Jacobs; creative writers like Rolfe and Alvah Bessie; as well as students from City College, NYU, Columbia, Cal Berkeley, and many other universities. And while many artists in the 1930s were content to permit their work to serve as a kind of weapon against fascism, many other artists actually went to war in Spain. Although they were few in

---

[101] Steven Jaffe, Peter N. Carroll & James D. Fernadez, *Facing Fascism: New York & The Spanish Civil War* (New York, NYU Press, 2007) 180.

[102] James Anderson, *The Spanish Civil War: A History and Reference Guide* (Westport, CT, Greenwood Press, 2003) 148.

[103] See Peter N. Carroll, *The Odyssey of the Abraham Lincoln Brigade: Americans in the Spanish Civil War* (Stanford, CA: Stanford University Press, 1994) 328.

number, artists amongst the American volunteers were certainly overrepresented in regard to society at large. Many were serious artists and painters who had exhibited their work, as well as composers, such as Ed Balchowsky, whose music had been performed, and writers, such as Rolfe, who had been published and widely read.[104]

By the time the Republic fell to Franco's fascists on April 1, 1939, as many as thirty-five National Artist Union members had gone to Spain as fighters, translators, drivers and nurses, and more than half were killed.[105] The AU members that stayed in the states

---

[104] Robert A. Rosenstone, "The Men of the Abraham Lincoln Battalion," *The Journal of American History*, Vol. 54, No. 2 (Sep., 1967), pp. 327-338. note 19

[105] A second important national artists' organization was the American Artists' Congress (AAC) founded in 1935 by leftist activists. Antifascism, opposition to racism, and support for Spain were high on the agenda. Unlike many other left/liberal magazines, *New Masses* was surprisingly supportive of visual arts; the editors reproduced not only political cartoons but also drawings, prints, and paintings in its pages, along with muckraking political analyses, contemporary fiction, and theater, music and art reviews. Artists and writers addressed varied social justice themes from parallel leftist perspectives. Artists faced few stylistic constraints and their representational choices ranged from proletarian realism to cubist and surrealist inspired modernism. Visual art placed next to text created a complementary resonance that intensified factual and emotional meanings and reinforced the significance of issues the journal wished to emphasize. Most of the workers reproduced in *New Masses* are now unlocated. Wealthy collectors did not usually want such works, and those exchanged among the artists themselves, or purchased by sympathetic leftist and liberal patrons, disappeared during the McCarthy Era or were discarded by heirs who did not recognize their value. These works tend to fall into several

actively raised funds to send two fully equipped ambulances, with its logo emblazoned on their sides, to the American base hospital outside Madrid. The AU also produced its own newspaper, *Art Front*, which published news, essays, and photos from the Spanish trenches, which became a significant source of information for artists who wanted to create projects that addressed the suffering and sacrifice that was so intricately part of the Spanish War, as well as Japan's invasion of China. Artists' activism during the war was often generated, in part, by their recent successes in

---

dominant categories: landscapes showing the terrible destruction of the Spanish countryside and peasant communities, images of women and children as the vulnerable civilian victims of military actions, works that valorize the brave commitment of peasant militias and IB troops, and those that enunciate American activist politics as artists protested aerial bombings in Spain and demanded that the arms embargo be lifted. Throughout the war the question of whether opposition to fascism required artists to spell out their political views in their works remained contentious. Stuart Davis, editor of *Art Front* insisted that abstraction in itself was a radical contribution to political change and disdained the idea that revolutionary art must literally illustrate revolutionary concepts or events. See Helen Langa in Peter N. Carroll & James D. Fernadez, *Facing Fascism: New York & The Spanish Civil War* (New York, NYU Press, 2007) 105 - 117. The images are often crudely drawn or "artless," echoing the crudeness or straightforwardness of the heroes portrayed in the various cartoons or magazine covers. The political icons are clearly represented, with the united proletariat consistently triumphing over fascism. The graphic arts themselves were seen by many at the time as more "democratic" than painting or sculpture, and thus more "proletarian." See Cecile Whiting, *Antifascism in American Art*, (New Haven and London: Yale University Press, 1989).

gaining Federal work relief through the establishment of the Works Progress Administration's Federal Art Project (WPA-FAP) in 1935, and in developing several militant organizations to demand fair treatment for these new federal workers and to promote democracy and artists' rights throughout the U.S.

Many politically-committed creative workers rejected the aesthetic of isolation that had characterized the "lost generation" of the 1920s. When the artist-volunteers went to Spain, it was often, as their letters indicate, to fulfill this ideal of camaraderie with the economically and politically oppressed people of the world. Rather than fleeing America and its discontents, very many Depression-era intellectuals and artists affirmed their identity with the so called masses, which was particularly evident in numerous WPA and AU projects produced during the War in Spain, and especially by the high-percentage of artists who risked life, limb and citizenship fighting fascism.

Usually individualistic (in theory anyway), many artists in the 1930s had become collective-minded during the Great Depression, banding together in various leagues and cooperatives. Their romanticism and idealism found outlets in the glorification of "the workers'" inherent struggles with managers. Many were inspired by the fateful purges of artists and intellectuals in Nazi Germany and had volunteered for service in Spain partly because they felt impotent in their normal roles, but largely because the human values upon which modern art depended seemed especially threatened by the frighteningly rapid expansion of fascist influence throughout the world.[106]

That so many American intellectuals supported the Spanish Republic underscored the ideological imperatives of the 1930s. Not only did left-wing artists and writers envision a society that would respect and encourage their artistic production; they also realized that inimical fascist doctrines threatened the essence of independent creativity. Many volunteers were, therefore, simultaneously idealists, anxious for a better world, and concomitantly realists, who understood acutely that their enemies aimed to set civilization back to the Dark Ages, i.e. pre-Enlightenment Era, in which slavery was the natural order. For many of the volunteers, especially the artists and scholars, Spain represented a watershed moment in human history in which failure would inevitably result in social, political and economic calamity for all the proverbial 1%.[107]

---

[106] Robert A. Rosenstone, "The Men of the Abraham Lincoln Battalion," *The Journal of American History*, Vol. 54, No. 2 (Sep., 1967), pp. 327-338, note 20

[107] Peter N. Carroll, *The Odyssey of the Abraham Lincoln Brigade: Americans in the Spanish Civil War* (Stanford, CA: Stanford University Press, 1994) 88.

Chapter Three

"Communism in the Great Depression"

During the first week of November 1936 – four months after the start of General Francisco Franco's military coup to topple Spain's democratically elected government – three Communist Party functionaries met in a small lower Manhattan office to discuss the formation of the American International Brigades, to which the Lincoln and Washington battalions would eventually belong.[108] Word of the new brigade spread, especially amongst members of the Popular Front in New York, Philadelphia, Chicago, San Francisco, and other heavily industrialized cities that were home to powerful labor organizations.

Since the American volunteers were prohibited to go to Spain, they had to first travel to France and be smuggled or sneaked into Spain. Passage to the French ports from New York was paid for by the Communist Party of the United States, but reimbursed by the Spanish Republic (except for a small number of stowaways and men crossing on their own). Once in France, volunteers passed into the custody of the Communist Party of France, which arranged passage to the central base of the International Brigades' at Albacete, Spain. At Albacete the majority of American volunteers went into the newly formed Fifteenth Battalion of the International Brigade, while the rest

---

[108] There were reportedly fifty-three (at least) nations represented in the International Brigades.

became medical orderlies, truck drivers, or base personnel.[109]

By the summer of 1937, nearly two thousand men, enough to form two battalions, had made their way to Spain. By then the ranks had opened to socialists, and sundry other liberals and idealists not necessarily affiliated with the Communist Party. The non-communists constituted about a third or more of the roughly three thousand Americans who eventually went to defend the Spanish Republic.[110] The organization of the International Brigades – from enlistment to passage – remained under Communist Party supervision. Every man accepted into what would eventually become the Lincoln Battalion had been, at least tacitly, approved by the CPUSA. But that does not necessarily mean that the individual was a dyed in the wool communist, and, furthermore, does not give credence to the notion that the Lincolns fought for "the hammer and sickle," as critics sometimes assailed. Carl Geiser, who was a member of the Communist Party, did not, for example, believe himself to be fighting to advance Bolshevism, but rather believed he was engaged in a struggle "between democracy and fascism, and not between

---

[109] Cecil D. Eby, *Comrades and Commissars: The Lincoln Battalion in the Spanish Civil War*, (University Park, Pa. The Pennsylvania State University Press, 2007).

[110] Peter N. Carroll & James D. Fernadez, *Facing Fascism: New York & The Spanish Civil War*, (New York, NYU, 2007) 14. It is to be noted that a few Americans were already serving with the POUM militia in Aragon. See Malcolm Cowley, "Lament for the Abraham Lincoln Battalion," *The Sewanee Review*, Vol. 92, No. 3 (Summer, 1984), pp. 331-347, xi.

communism and fascism or democracy."[111] Though the International Brigades were organized by the

---

[111] Carl Geiser Papers, ALBA.004, Folder: Outgoing Correspondence, May 9, 1937, Albacete, Spain. Geiser was born in Orrville, Ohio on December 10, 1910. He was the oldest of six children; his father, a farmer, died in the influenza epidemic at the end of World War I, and his mother a year later of tuberculosis. His maternal grandparents, Swiss immigrants who spoke little English, raised Geiser and his siblings. The young Geiser received his primary education in a one-room schoolhouse while helping to tend the family's sixteen-acre farm. Upon his graduation from Orrville High School in 1928, he enrolled in the YMCA School of Technology (later Fenn College) in Cleveland, where he majored in electrical engineering. In 1932, following the establishment of diplomatic relations between the United States and the Soviet Union, Geiser was part of the first National Student Federation mission to travel to the newly recognized country. This visit had a decisive influence on shaping Geiser's political thinking. Impressed by the Soviet system and the tenets of socialist ideology, Geiser joined the Young Communist League upon his return to Ohio. He became an active force in the American Student Union in Cleveland and served as a delegate to the First Student Congress Against War and Fascism held in Chicago. It was there that Geiser met his future wife Sylvia, a teacher and organizer who shared his political fervor. The couple moved to New York where they were absorbed into a dynamic culture of political activism and organizing. Geiser wrote press releases and edited International Labor Defense bulletins, organized for the League against War and Fascism, and in 1936 was elected to the National Committee of the Young Communist League. On April 13, 1937 Geiser boarded the *S.S. Georgic* to join the International Brigades massing in defense of the Spanish Republic. He served as an ammunition carrier at the Battle of Brunete, saw action at Quinto, and advanced to the rank of Lieutenant. Following the Battle of Belchite in September 1937, Geiser was promoted to Political Commissar and charged with the organization of a training school for commissars at Tarazona. Wounded at the conflict at Fuentes de Ebro, Geiser was hospitalized for three months. Returned to the front as Commissar of the Mackenzie-Papineau Battalion in January 1938, he was captured by fascist forces on April 1, 1938. For the next year, he was interned at

Communist Party, volunteers were also not actually paid by the Soviet Union; they were paid by the Spanish Republic and from donations provided by sympathetic supporters. Neither the Communist Party in Moscow nor the CPUSA had any intention or means of dipping into its coffers to underwrite the volunteers' sense of idealism.[112] Though Communists did lead the way in organizing the committees and congresses, and the international units as well, those who joined the committees and went to rallies sympathetic to the Republic were not, for the most part, seeking to advance a Bolshevik cause. They were guided, not so much by political ideology, but rather by a sense of idealism especially pronounced during the poignant and painful social and economic despair of the Great Depression.

One thing all American volunteers had in common was a confrontation with the Great Depression. Though there were some well-to-do American

---

San Pedro de Cardeña, along with over 650 International Brigades prisoners. Through the efforts of the Friends of the Abraham Lincoln Brigade and the U.S. State Department, Geiser and a group of 71 Americans were released in April 1939. Geiser returned to New York and secured an engineering position with Liquidometer, a manufacturer of aeronautic equipment. Working with the company in various capacities for the next 40 years, Geiser filed numerous patents and, as a research director, supervised the testing of a component used in the first lunar mission. He also served briefly as president of Local 1227 of the United Electrical Radio and Machine Workers of America. SACB, Cadre, RA, USSDA 2:0574; ALBA 004 Carl Geiser Papers Audio Collection, POW, Harriman, Carl Geiser, *Prisoners of the Good Fight*.

[112] Cecil Eby, *Between the Bullet and the Lie: American Volunteers in the Spanish Civil War*, (San Francisco, Holt, Rhinehart and Winston, 1969) 5.

volunteers, most of them were products of working-class backgrounds. Many had known deprivation and joblessness long before the stock market cratered in 1929. Many of the American volunteers thus felt considerable solidarity with the international working class, and many knew the shame and humiliation of being desperate for work. As such, when military officers, strongly supported by wealthy landowners, rebelled against the Spanish Republic's democratically elected Popular Front government, many American volunteers recognized it as part of a Depression-era struggle against wealth and power already being waged in their own hometowns. Conservative critics of the American volunteers for the Republic of Spain also often perceived Spain to be relational to battles between workers and employers in the U.S. and thus vilified their idealism by assailing their military service in Spain by reducing their courage to them simply being naïve dupes of Stalin.

Additionally, although the Comintern organized the International Brigades, it did so surreptitiously; therefore evidence that an American fought in Spain cannot be used to prove that he was at that time or subsequently, a member of the Communist Party or a communist sympathizer. No less an authority than the Subversive Activities Control Board, which investigated the alleged connection during the McCarthy Era, made the point clear in its 1955 report, stating: "The record shows that some Americans fought there on behalf of the Republic out of motivations alien to communist purposes."[113]

---

[113] Ibid, xxi.

It is also important to note that some American volunteers who had joined a communist organization did so simply to get to Spain.[114] For many American volunteers, politics were of secondary importance; their decision to volunteer was determined more by personal experiences that shaped their idealism rather than politics.[115] Don McLeod's working-class family, for instance, had been throttled by the Great Depression. Except for being influenced by writers such as Upton Sinclair, he described himself as largely apolitical. "To tell you the truth," he remembered, "I don't think I had ever read a single word of Karl Marx or even had heard of him by the time I joined the Young Communist League. And the only reason I did so was because I was told that you had a better chance of getting to Spain if you belonged."[116]

Other volunteers distanced themselves from the party soon after arriving in Spain. "You have probably noticed that since I left Paris I have lost some of the rank-and-file tendencies that I had there and before leaving the states," Dartmouth graduate Joe Dallet wrote his wife. "The situation does not permit having them

---

[114] Hank Rubin, foreword by Peter N. Carroll, *Spain's Cause Was Mine: A Memoir of an American Medic in the Spanish Civil War* (Carbondale, Southern Illinois University Press, 1997) xv.

[115] Fraser Ottanelli in Peter N. Carroll & James D. Fernadez, *Facing Fascism: New York & The Spanish Civil War* (New York, NYU Press, 2007) 65.

[116] Don McLeod as quoted in John Gerassi, *The Premature Antifascists: North American Volunteers in the Spanish Civil War 1936-39: An Oral History* (New York, Praeger, 1986) 49. McLeod went to Santa Barbara State College for two years before transferring to California Berkeley.

and it's a question of jumping in wherever you can do the most good, no matter what your personal inclination might be."[117]

In Spain, American volunteers were especially recalcitrant to Soviet leadership, which many Lincolns perceived to be incompetent. They often recoiled at discipline, except the sort imposed from within their own ranks, which especially demonstrates a lack of allegiance to anything but their ideals. Their aversion to the pomp and circumstance of military discipline from non-American commanders who had not earned their respect subjected them to harsh treatment by Soviet leaders who considered them spoiled Americans. Many American volunteers were especially resented by Soviet leadership for their aversion to saluting officers. "There was no reason we should salute," seaman Bill Bailey remembered. "So what if you were a commissar, or officer, or lieutenant? A bullet doesn't discriminate. We respected a guy because he was a good guy; not because of a couple of bars."[118]

---

[117] Albacete, May 3, 1937, Joe Dallet, "Letters From Spain, American Volunteer to His Wife" (New York, Workers Library Publishers, 1938). 37. Vertical files box 2, folder 60. Elmer Holmes Tamiment Library, 70 Washington Square South, New York NY 10012, New York University Libraries.

[118] Bill Bailey as quoted in Noel Buckner, Mary Dore, and Sam Sills' *The Good Fight: The Abraham Lincoln Brigade in the Spanish Civil War*, 1984. Bailey was born in 1909 Hoboken, New Jersey. He was the son of Irish immigrants. In 1935 he removed the Nazi flag flying over the S.S. Bremen and was arrested and beaten, though eventually acquitted of the charges. Before going to Spain he was a longshoremen and seaman. He fought with the Seamen's machine-gun company. He was blacklisted during the Korean War due to his involvement with the Communist Party. He died in San Francisco in 1995. See also

Many American volunteers were, in fact, as Dallet's correspondence to his wife reveal, devoutly non-ideological. Many others who were communists ceased to be during the war, when Stalin's Show Trial atrocities began to come to light, and especially when he allied the Soviet Union with Adolf Hitler's Third Reich and divided Poland in two. Many American volunteers never identified themselves as communists at all. But the majority of volunteers, probably three quarters or more in the case of New York, did in fact come from within the Popular Front sphere of influence, which is not necessarily synonymous with being a communist.

The notion that the American volunteers were "fighting for communism," as critics asserted, is largely hollow and empty Culture War rhetoric espoused by demagogues such as Father Charles Coughlin and quasi-fascists such as J. Edgar Hoover, both of whom pejoratively reduced the American volunteers' complex human thoughts, emotions, experiences, and idealism in order to vilify them as political enemies. The fact is, many American volunteers were – as their wartime letters demonstrate – idealists above all else who had come of age during the Great Depression. "I knew about oppression," American volunteer Ed Balchowsky, who lost an arm fighting for the Spanish Republic, said. Going to Spain "didn't take any effort or thinking. I didn't need any politics. They were oppressed – the Spanish people – so I knew what that meant. So I wanted to go help."[119] His compatriot, Milt Wolfe, who

---

Malcolm Cowley, "Lament for the Abraham Lincoln Battalion" *The Sewanee Review*, Vol. 92, No. 3 (Summer, 1984), pp. 331-347.

[119] Ed Balchowsky as quoted in Noel Buckner, Mary Dore, and Sam Sills' *The Good Fight: The Abraham Lincoln*

had a respected career as a writer and civil rights activist in the decades after the Spanish War, likewise remembered that, "we weren't fighting under the orders of the Communist Party or for the Comintern, but or the Spanish people."[120] Salaria Key, an African American

---

Brigade in the Spanish Civil War, 1984. Balchowsky was born in 1916. He sailed November 6, 1937 aboard the *Lafayette*. He returned in December 1938 aboard the *President Harding*. His right arm was amputated after being wounded in the Ebro Offensive. Even after the injury he was a renowned pianist and artist who performed in clubs in Chicago. Some of his artwork was displayed in Oprah Winfrey's restaurant. Tom McNamee, "Chicago Loses an Original," *Chicago Sun Times*, December 4, 1989.

[120] Milt Wolff as quoted in Noel Buckner, Mary Dore, and Sam Sills' *The Good Fight: The Abraham Lincoln Brigade in the Spanish Civil War*, 1984. Born in Brooklyn on October 8, 1915, Wolff stood six feet two in bare feet and a few inches higher in the muddied brown boots he had picked up after swimming across the swollen Ebro River during the great retreats of 1938, just a few months before Hemingway wrote his profile. He had a loud, gravelly voice that was pure Brooklyn. Later, he claimed that was the reason he was picked to lead the Lincoln volunteers at the age of 22, but Wolff knew (he always knew but it embarrassed him) that he possessed a tremendous charisma that won the love of men and women throughout his life. And what all of them also knew was that Milton Wolff was a very intelligent man. He sailed for Spain in March 1937. Wolff recounted his experiences as a soldier in the autobiographical novel, Another Hill (1994). Moved by the enthusiasm of the other volunteers, he switched from a medical assignment to serve in a machine gun company in the newly formed Washington Battalion and went into action at Brunete in July 1937. Men inches away from him were wounded and killed, but he emerged without a nick. A few weeks later, while on leave in Madrid, his captain, Philip Detro from Texas steered him to the Cafe Chicote on the Gran Via. There he met Ernest Hemingway. The 21-year old Wolff was not impressed. "Ernest is quite childish in many respects," he wrote to a friend in Brooklyn. "He wants very much to be a martyr. So much for writers," he concluded. "I'd much rather

read their works than be with them." Within a month, Wolff was fighting on the Aragon front, leading a section of the machine gun company at Belchite and Quinto. By October, he commanded the machine gunners at Fuentes de Ebro. At Teruel, in January 1938, Wolff was a captain and an adjutant. Two months later, when a direct hit destroyed the battalion headquarters and killed the leadership, Wolff became the commander. He led the soldiers through the treacherous retreats, avoided capture, and wandered alone behind enemy lines until managing to swim across the Ebro. Wolff assumed responsibility for rebuilding the broken battalion. During the training period, Robert Capa, the legendary photographer, captured Wolff standing next to Hemingway, a visual contradiction: Hemingway, stocky, an adventurer in his half-opened zippered jacket; Wolff, lanky in uniform, a beret covering his thick, dark hair, but shy, hands in his pockets, face turned downward, impatient to get on with the war. A few weeks later, the photograph appeared in a New York Yiddish newspaper. To her surprise, Wolff's mother finally discovered what her absent son was doing in Spain. Not, as he had reported in his letters, working in a factory so that a Spanish worker could fight for the Republic, but leapfrogging through the military ranks. A "nobody at home," the soldier-poet Edwin Rolfe wrote about Wolff in his diary: "leader of men here." Wolff led the Lincolns back across the Ebro during the summer of 1938, held them in the lines of the violent Hill 666 in the Sierra Pandols, until ordered to turn over the battalion to Spanish officers as the government arranged for the withdrawal of foreign troops in 1938. In a ceremonial transfer of authority, Wolff was promoted to the rank of Major. After Spain Wolff's iconic stature kept him at the forefront of the struggle to save the Spanish Republic, even after General Francisco Franco claimed military victory in 1939. He participated in street protests in New York, urging Washington officials to lift the embargo on shipments to Spain and to provide assistance for the Spanish refugees trapped in French concentration camps. When the French government threatened to deport these victims of war back to Franco's Spain, where many would face summary execution, Wolff joined other Lincoln veterans in demonstrations outside the French consulate in New York. He was arrested in 1940 for this activity and served fifteen days in jail. As the anti-Communist crusade abated in the 1960s, Wolff remained active in the U.S.

nurse who volunteered, likewise remembered that she went to Spain not to help communism, but rather as a medical professional dedicated to helping victimized and oppressed people. "Look at all these children being bombed," she said. "I was doing Christ's duty."[121] A similar sentiment was especially expressed by nurse Federika Martin. Her papers in the Abraham Lincoln Brigade archive at New York University contain hundreds of correspondences between her and other medical professionals, friends and family. But almost none of her words allude to political ideology. What is especially prominent in her correspondence, however, is a genuine concern to help people in need of medical attention who would otherwise be deprived of it.

Committee for a Democratic Spain, an organization that lobbied against U.S. treaties with the Franco regime, assisted the families of Franco's political prisoners, and advocated for political reform. Wolff also led the revitalized VALB in demonstrations against the Vietnam War. At one point, he wrote a personal letter to Ho Chi Minh offering the services of the Abraham Lincoln Brigade. He also advocated ending the trade embargo with Cuba and helped provide medical aid to a children's hospital in Havana. During the 1980s, Wolff and other veterans instituted a campaign to send ambulances to Nicaragua, an echo of U.S. domestic support for the Spanish Republic fifty years earlier. Invited frequently to return to Spain, Wolff was a beloved figure among Spaniards. In a recent visit, he won cheers when he reminded them that if they got into trouble in the future, "give me a call." Excerpts from Milton Wolff's obituary by Peter N. Carroll; http://www.alba-valb.org/volunteers/milton-wolff.

[121] Salaria Key as quoted in Noel Buckner, Mary Dore, and Sam Sills' *The Good Fight: The Abraham Lincoln Brigade in the Spanish Civil War*, 1984. Key was born in Georgia. Her father was a worker in a sanitarium. After her father was killed by a patient, her mother moved the family to Akron, Ohio. She moved to Harlem in 1930 to become a nurse. She left for Spain aboard the *Paris* on March 27, 1937.

Perhaps deep down she was, in fact, motivated by politics and/or ideology, but her letters simply do not betray anything but a genuine concern to help people in need.

Some American volunteers even criticized Russia in letters home from Spain. "There is a feeling of class consciousness (in Spain) I think you would find in no other country," Henry Plotnick wrote in 1937, "and I am not excluding Russia. For Russia is almost a generation removed from her basic struggle against imperialism."[122] Paul Wendorf, a historian and economist trained at Columbia University, likewise lamented in a letter home that:

> "The *Daily (Worker)* at times has been pretty childish in reporting war news, as if it were a great big picnic with the fascists running as soon as we showed our noses. I think the reason is that the fellows at the desk in New York use their imaginations too freely in writing up brief cable messages. I've also acquired what I consider a healthy proletarian prejudice against the guys who think their importance to the world is in rhapsodizing over the struggles of others… I think that sympathy and support will be won on a much more solid basis if we present things just as they are.[123]

---

[122] As quoted by Henry Plotnick Murcia, Spain, 1937, in Marcel Acier, ed, *From Spanish Trenches: Recent Letters From Spain* (New York, Modern Age, 1937) 159. Plotnick was born March 9, 1915. The Brooklyn native attended City College of New York. He arrived in Spain March 27, 1937.

[123] Paul Wendorf, Box 1, Folder: October/November 1937, Tamiment Library/Robert F. Wagner Labor Archives.

Plotnik and Wendorf's sober criticism underscores the fact that the volunteers were not dupes or automatons; they were individualistic Americans and devout idealists. Many of the Lincolns were, like McLeod, more likely to cite as formative political influences *All Quiet on the Western Front* than *Das Kapital* or the *Daily Worker*. Very many volunteers belonged to

---

Elmer Holmes Tamiment Library, 70 Washington Square South, New York NY 10012, New York University Libraries. Wendorf graduated with a B.A. from Columbia University, where he majored in history and economics, in 1932. In 1933, while working as an organizer for the American League against War and Fascism, he joined the Communist Party. Over the course of the next three years, he worked as an activist and labor organizer in New York City, first for a white-collar municipal workers' union, and subsequently as a coordinator of welfare and relief for the unemployed. He married Leona Grossman and soon after enlisted in the Abraham Lincoln Brigade to fight on behalf of the Republican forces in Spain. He sailed on the *S.S. Paris* on February 6, 1937 and served in Spain from February 1937 until August 1938. He fought in the battle at the Jarama front from March to June 1937, and in the Brunete offensive from July until August 1937. He was appointed in September 1937 to the Historical Commission in Albacete and, under the supervision of Sandor Voros, participated in writing the history of the 15th International Brigade and the American battalions. He also contributed articles to the Brigade's newspaper the *Volunteer for Liberty*. In January of 1938 he was charged, along with Carl Geiser, with organizing a school for political commissars. A bout of rheumatism and subsequent hospitalization prevented him from carrying out this assignment, and by March, he was returned to active service. He took part in the Ebro offensive, the Brigade's final conflict, and crossed the Ebro with the Lincoln Brigade late in July. On August 18, 1938, Wendorf was killed during an aerial attack in the Sierra Pandols, only one month prior to the withdrawal of the International Brigades.

no political party, referring to themselves as simply "anti-fascists."[124]

Whether self-described as a communist, socialist, liberal, or simply apolitical, most volunteers for the Spanish Republic seemed to agree that the rapid rise of fascism in Europe was a grave threat to western civilization and the principles associated with the Enlightenment, namely liberty, equality and fraternity – all of which seemed especially threatened by the economic turmoil part and parcel of the Great Depression.   As such, to really understand why American volunteers were willing to risk life, limb and citizenship to aid the Republic of Spain in its war with fascist rebels, it is important to acknowledge the widespread suffering and social despair of the Depression, a time when millions of Americans were chronically unemployed, despite the reforms of the first and second New Deal; violent struggles to organize industrial labor unions had also exacerbated class distinctions; there was widespread disillusionment with capitalism among many American intellectuals, which informed a growing interest in Marxism; the rise of Italian fascism and German Nazism, which, in Europe, had smashed labor unions, persecuted minorities, and purged artists and intellectuals who dared criticize the glaring inequity in distribution of political and economic resources, and was also especially central to the political climate in the U.S., especially amongst hyphenated Americans; the rising undercurrent of totalitarianism within the United States as demagogues like Father

---

[124] Robert A. Rosenstone, "The Men of the Abraham Lincoln Battalion," *The Journal of American History*, Vol. 54, No. 2 (Sep., 1967), pp. 327-338.

Coughlin claimed millions of followers, and the Silver Shirts, who aped Hitler and Mussolini's fascist tactics, all helped inspire a resurgent leftist ethos in contrast to the fascistic elements in American popular culture during the Depression.

It is equally important to underscore the fact that, in the decades before the Cold War, the Popular Front of the 1930s was incredibly attuned to the main themes of American civil society, and was even supporting the New Deal. Meanwhile, its internal organization had become more flexible, especially in contrast to the rigidity of the Democratic and Republican parties, both of which were predominately anti-black. American Communists had departed a bit from the militancy that characterized Josef Stalin's Soviet Union, and were even sponsoring cocktail parties, dances, and moonlight cruises up the Hudson River to facilitate exchanges of ideas and stoke party membership.[125]

It is also crucial to underscore the point that millions of Americans in the 1930s were concomitantly disenchanted with the Republican and Democratic parties because poverty, fear, unemployment, and demoralization were widespread, and because many blamed the two-party system for failing to prevent and/or end the Great Depression. By the start of the war in Spain the lines of the unemployed in American cities teemed; wages were stagnant, and in many cases falling for those lucky enough to keep their jobs, and every day more businesses closed their doors; factories were increasingly boarded and abandoned and there were scores of families vacating the failed farms of the

---

[125] Ibid, pp. 327-338.

Midwest Dust Bowl and trying to escape despair by migrating to states such as California and Florida. Among American youths there was a "sense of alienation from the establishment," Hank Rubin wrote in his memoir, "for we had nowhere to go, little hope of meaningful jobs, or, if we were employed, little chance for security or advancement."[126]

In truth, many American volunteers were, in fact, affiliated with the CPUSA during the Great Depression. But those who were members of CPUSA-affiliated organizations were perhaps not quite as guilty of being naïve and/or malevolent as were the two major political parties in the U.S., with respect to addressing the most important international and domestic issues of the decade, particularly the social inequity part and parcel of economic inequity.[127] James Phillip Lardner, a war correspondent, the son of the famous performer Ring Lardner, and former Harvard student, who ultimately volunteered to fight fascism (and died) in Spain, poignantly defended himself against red baiting by his mother in a July 1938 letter:

> It is not the goal of the Communist Party in any country to establish socialism or communism by violent overthrow of the government. The communists are working everywhere, as openly as any party in the world, to win the people to

---

[126] Hank Rubin, foreword by Peter N. Carroll, *Spain's Cause Was Mine: A Memoir of an American Medic in the Spanish Civil War* (Carbondale, Southern Illinois University Press, 1997) 7.

[127] Peter N. Carroll, *The Odyssey of the Abraham Lincoln Brigade: Americans in the Spanish Civil War* (Stanford, CA: Stanford University Press, 1994) 63.

their way of thinking by peaceful, organizational methods. They are convinced, however, from experience, that they can never accomplish this without running into armed opposition from the reactionaries, the capitalists, the imperialists, and now the fascists. And they must be prepared for this opposition. The virulent, slanderous, small-minded, biased, contemptible characterizations of communists as dirty, bomb-throwing foreigners, etc., which you have heard your share of, are ridiculous. The Communists are a good deal more democratic than the Democrats or the Republicans and everything they stand for in the United States has been publicized over and over. If you think they stand for one thing in public and another in private, then 75,000 members of the party are being consistently duped.[128]

It is also important to note that prior to the Cold War the Soviet Union was not yet imperialistic; it was struggling to gain national recognition and allies above all else. "We repudiate the reckless resolve to seize power by any minority," CPUSA leader Earl Browder wrote in 1938. "The Communist Party represents a strong and growing force to support and help every progressive tendency in American political life, and in no case to

---

[128] James Lardner, July 6, 1938, SRI, 17.1, Barcelona. In Lardner Papers, ALBA.067, Folder: Letters, Tamiment Library/Robert F. Wagner Labor Archives. Elmer Holmes Tamiment Library, 70 Washington Square South, New York NY 10012, New York University Libraries.

distract the progressive People's Front from its fight against reactionaries and fascists."[129]

At a time when Browder was struggling to define communism as "twentieth century Americanism," and when the party was effectively supporting the New Deal, the appeal of the ideology was its practical critique of capitalism's structural flaws and the party's subsequent struggle for unemployment relief, better conditions for blue-collar workers, and opposition to fascism.

Also, by the mid-1930s, domestic developments in the United States and international pressure made the CPUSA set aside its emphasis on revolution to embrace a policy known as the "Popular Front," which was based on a broad alliance with socialist and liberal forces in defense of democratic institutions against the rising tide of Fascism around the world.[130] In the 1930s American Communists were, in short, above all, and perhaps more than any political group, social activists.[131] The CPUSA's anti-fascism especially mirrored the perceptions of a growing number of politically active liberals, noncommunist left-wingers, and unionists who provided the basis for the formation of the North

---

[129] Earl Browder and Bill Lawrence, *Next Steps to Win the War in Spain*, (New York, Workers Library Publishers, January 1938) 11.

[130] Steven Jaffe in Peter N. Carroll & James D. Fernadez, *Facing Fascism: New York & The Spanish Civil War* (New York, NYU Press, 2007) 179.

[131] Justin Byrne in Peter N. Carroll & James D. Fernadez, *Facing Fascism: New York & The Spanish Civil War* (New York, NYU Press, 2007) 80.

American Committee to Aid Spanish Democracy, which was the most important and largest organization in support of democratic Spain. The CPUSA was also the organization most actively involved in support of the Spanish loyalists, who had been democratically elected. The Communists, as even George Orwell (a Trotskyist) admitted, did get on with the war in Spain.

Frustrated by the failure of the free world to assist the Republic, many volunteers became convinced that only communism and Soviet Russia stood as bulwarks against the spread of fascism throughout the world.[132] The "neutrality" of England, France and the United States especially justified American volunteers' concerns, thereby pushing many idealists to the left. The western empires' non-intervention policies were integral to the fall of Spain to Franco's rebels and the subsequent rise of World War II, which cost tens of millions of lives around the world.

Besides, so what if the volunteers were communists? The great lure of communism during the Great Depression was its idealism, especially as contrasted to the cynicism of capitalism, which had plunged the entire world into economic calamity and set the stage for the rise of fascism.[133] Also, in hindsight, the maturation of industrialized capitalism also fueled British, American, and French imperialism, which was

---

[132] Victor Hoar, "In Our Time: The Abraham Lincoln Brigade and the Historians," *American Quarterly*, Vol. 22, No. 1 (Spring, 1970), pp. 112-119.

[133] Peter N. Carroll, *The Odyssey of the Abraham Lincoln Brigade: Americans in the Spanish Civil War* (Stanford, CA: Stanford University Press, 1994) 63.

as much a cause of World War II as was the reparations clause in the Treaty of Versailles. "In these pre-World War II years, the American Left," Hank Rubin wrote in his memoir, "seemed to be the only segment of our political culture that was as worried about fascism. The Communist slogan, 'From each according to his ability and to each according to his needs,' sounded more rational, more kind, and more like the philosophy of a society I could respect."[134]

During America's political struggles in the 1930's, communist activism proved a great asset in winning economic benefits for the unemployed and homeless. Communists also established a fine and honorable record of opposing racial injustice; the party was virtually the only predominately white political organization of its time to accept blacks on equal terms. A black Lincoln named James Yates explained his affinity for the Communist Party as the only political organization in the U.S. that recognized "the reality of my life," the dual oppression of race and class.[135] By 1936, tens of thousands of Americans were, indeed,

---

[134] Hank Rubin, foreword by Peter N. Carroll, *Spain's Cause Was Mine: A Memoir of an American Medic in the Spanish Civil War* (Carbondale, Southern Illinois University Press, 1997) 16 and 18.

[135] James Yates, Mississippi to Madrid: Memoir of a Black American in the Abraham Lincoln Brigade (Greensboro, NC, Open Hand Publishing, 1989) 97. Yates was born in Mississippi in 1906. He moved to Chicago as a teenager, where he found work in meatpacking plants. He was active in unemployment councils and the Scotsboro defense campaign. He moved to New York to find work in the 1930s, where he became involved in Communist organizations. He arrived in France aboard the *Ile de France* in February 1937 and returned to the U.S. a year later aboard the Lafayette due to illness. He served in the Army during World War II.

Communists because the party seemed to be a radical alternative to the rapaciousness and greed associated with the casino capitalism that had created the Great Depression.

Communism in 1930s America had not yet, in short, been ubiquitously demonized as it would later become during the Cold War witch hunts and blacklists insisted upon by fascistic elements in the U.S. government, personified by Senator Martin Dies, Senator Joseph McCarthy, and the Federal Bureau of Investigation's J. Edgar Hoover.

Whether Harvard grads or dockworkers, many Communists in the 1930s had embraced the ideology because America was severely depressed economically, which exacerbated social inequity throughout the nation. During the Great Depression it seemed evident to many millions of Americans, including scores of devout non-communists, that the capitalist system was, in fact, the antithesis of egalitarian ideals popularized during the Enlightenment, and which ultimately inspired the American Revolution. Thus, many American volunteers rightly perceived the Spanish War to be a watershed moment in world history in which humanity would either progress towards greater economic and social equality, or else be pulled back into the Dark Ages by the likes of Franco, Hitler, Mussolini, Hoover and Coughlin.

Chapter Four

"The Longue Durée of Revolutions from Enlightenment to Spain"

In the words of Karl Marx, the French Revolution represented "the victory of bourgeois ownership over feudal ownership, of nationality over provincialism, of competition over the guild, of the division of land over primogeniture, of the rule of the landowner over the domination of the owner by the land, of enlightenment over superstition, of the family over the family name, of industry over heroic idleness, of bourgeois law over medieval privileges."[136] Such was the case – at least initially – in the French, American, and Russian Revolutions, as well as the rise of the Spanish Republic's Cortes prior to the counter-revolution sponsored by militarist fascists, including Adolf Hitler, Benito Mussolini and Francisco Franco.

The loyalist government of Spain was supported by nearly three thousand American volunteers and millions of other working and middle class Americans ideologically aligned with the cause because it was thought to be legal, constitutional, republican, liberal and democratic – i.e., consonant with the values associated with the American Revolution, which was heavily influenced by Enlightenment Era discourse.[137]

---

[136] See Peter McPhee, "The French Revolution, Peasants, and Capitalism" *The American Historical Review*, Vol. 94, No. 5 (Dec., 1989), pp. 1265-1280.

[137] Isaac Deutscher, the author of *Marx and Russia* (1948) in fact, declared that "Russia was the France of the new age," from which he expected "another 1789;" that is, a bourgeois and anti-feudal rather than socialist revolution. Since the Age of Enlightenment, Russian intellectuals had

Petitions were signed, speeches were delivered, and lives were risked not for the cause of Bolshevism... but for a faith in the movements that had dealt with George III and Louis XVI. Depression Era fascism," Eric Hobsbawm wrote in 2007, "was opposed in principle to the causes that defined and mobilized intellectuals," particularly the "values of the Enlightenment and the American and French Revolutions."

Spain, in short, seemed to many American volunteers and European intellectuals, such as Hobsbawm, to be the last chance for a representative government and pluralistic society in a Europe that had turned with horrifying speed toward dictatorship and totalitarianism. At a time when militant fascism defined the unreasonable, the Spanish Republic seemed to represent the Enlightenment's faith in reason as the faculty by which human beings have natural right to govern themselves without the threat of tyranny. For many American volunteers and their supporters, the Spanish Republic was, to be sure, symbolic of free speech, a free press, the right of assembly, the separation of Church and state, minority rights, and most especially

---

promoted Enlightenment ideals such as the dignity of the individual and the rectitude of democratic representation. These ideals were championed most vociferously by Russia's liberals, although populists, Marxists, and anarchists also claimed to support democratic reforms. Isaac Deutscher, *Russia in Transition* (New York, Kessinger, 1957), 166. See also George Comninel notes that in perhaps no other area of historical research has Marxian theory been so dominant among Western scholars. See George Comninel, *Rethinking the French Revolution: Marxism and the Revisionist Challenge* (London, Verso, 1987).

liberty, equality and fraternity.[138] Millions of Americans, volunteers for the Republic of Spain in particular, seemed honestly to have believed in the ideal of a fundamentally decent and reasonable people making steady progress under representative institutions. In that sense, as much as they were fighting in what is erroneously referred to as the Spanish "Civil War," the clash between fascism embodied by Franco, Hitler, and Mussolini and Spain, which was emblematic of representative government, was a continuation of the American, French, and Russian Revolutions, as were the subsequent revolutions in Latin America and Asia.[139] For

---

[138] It was only under the Third Republic that the motto was made official. During the German occupation of France in World War II, this motto was replaced by the reactionary phrase "travail, famille, patrie" (work, family, fatherland). Many other nations have adopted the French slogan of "liberty, equality, and fraternity" as an ideal. These words appear in the preamble to the Constitution of India, enforced in 1950. Since its founding, "Liberty, Equality and Brotherhood" has been the lemma of the Social Democratic Party of Denmark. In the United Kingdom the political party the Liberal Democrats refer to "the fundamental values of liberty, equality and community" in the preamble of the party's Federal Constitution, and this is printed on party membership cards. The idea of the slogan "Liberty, Equality, Fraternity" has also given an influence as natural law to the First Article of the Universal Declaration of Human Rights: All human beings are born free and equal in dignity and rights. They are endowed with reason and conscience and should act towards one another in a spirit of brotherhood. See Ozouf, Mona (1997), "Liberté, égalité, fraternité stands for peace country and war" in Nora, Pierre, Lieux de Mémoire (Places of memory) tome III, Quarto Gallimard, pp. 4353-89 (abridged translation, Realms of Memory, Columbia University Press, 1996-98).

[139] Historians such as Bernard Bailyn, Gordon Wood, and Edmund Morgan accept the contemporary view of the participants that the American Revolution was a unique and

many American volunteers, the Spanish Revolution of 1931, which toppled a monarchy, was another 1641 or 1789 or – most commonly – 1776.[140]

By the 1930s, the American and French Revolutions had helped inspire revolutions around the world, including in Cuba, the Philippines, Mexico, Russia, and many other counties.[141] Paul Wendorf, a historian and economist from Columbia, who volunteered to fight fascism in Spain, wrote in a letter to his wife that the first anniversary of the Defense of Madrid coincided with the twentieth anniversary of the Russian Revolution.[142]

---

radical event that produced deep changes and had a profound effect on world affairs, based – building on debates in the seventeenth-century English Civil War and subsequently – on an increasing belief in the principles of the Enlightenment, as reflected in how liberalism was understood during the period, and republicanism. These were demonstrated by a leadership and government that espoused protection of natural rights, and a system of laws chosen by the people.

[140] Allen Guttmann, *The Wound in the Heart: America and the Spanish Civil War* (New York, The Free Press/Macmillan, 1962) 4 and 206; Ezra Pound and others hoped that the death of the Republic would be followed by the rebirth of a nationalistic and an aristocratic social order, 201

[141] For a good perspective on revolutions throughout the world from the eighteenth century through post-World War II era of post-colonialism see Wim Kloosters, *Revolutions in the Atlantic World: A Comparative History* (New York, NYU Press, 2009).

[142] Paul Wendorf Papers, ALBA.120, Box 1, Folder: October/November 1937. Letter dated November 7, 1937. Tamiment Library/Robert F. Wagner Labor Archives. Elmer

Dartmouth graduate Joe Dallet explained his reasons for going to Spain in a letter to his mother in which he dialectically connected the American and French Revolution to 1930s Spain:

> Here is a war that MUST be won if peace and democracy are to have a chance to prevail… If I should happen to be one of those who falls, you can have the satisfaction of knowing that I fell in the most important battle in the world – the battle of democracy against Fascism – and that in volunteering and fighting I am following out the best traditions of world liberalism and democracy. Without the help of the gallant Lafayette, and his men, we would not today be the free USA. Without the help of the young American Republican, French Democracy could not have been successfully established. The free, democratic nations MUST unite against the fascist oppressors, and if to the ever-lasting shame of our fine national traditions the Roosevelt government helps the fascists rather than the friendly Spanish government, than right-thinking Americans must try to make up for this by their own actions.[143]

The American Revolution demonstrated to many volunteers that it was plausible for Enlightenment ideas

---

Holmes Tamiment Library, 70 Washington Square South, New York NY 10012, New York University Libraries.

[143] Joe Dallet Papers, ALBA.032, Box 1, folder: 1937. Letter dated March 19, 1937, Paris, France. Tamiment Library/Robert F. Wagner Labor Archives. Elmer Holmes Tamiment Library, 70 Washington Square South, New York NY 10012, New York University Libraries.

about how a government should be organized to actually be put into practice. Some American diplomats, like Benjamin Franklin and Thomas Jefferson, had lived in Paris where they consorted freely with members of the French intellectual class. Furthermore, contact between American revolutionaries and the French troops who served with the Colonial Army in North America helped spread revolutionary ideas to the French people and throughout the Atlantic World.[144] In other words, the American and French Revolutions fed each other, much like those two revolutions triggered others in subsequent generations.

Many International volunteers, including many Americans, were a kind of redux to the sans-culottes – commoners in late-eighteenth century France that rebelled against the Church and Monarchy. The sans-culottes' struggle was, like the majority of Spanish people in the twentieth century, in large part inspired by their poor quality of life under the *Ancien Régime*. The most fundamental political ideals of the sans-culottes were, like those expressed in many of the American volunteers' letters, social equality, economic

---

[144] Our age has been powerfully impressed by the economic interpretation of history proposed by Marxists; but it has also witnessed the important role played by men of letters and men of thought in the Spanish Civil War and in the Resistance movement of World War II. The problem of the effect of the Philosophy of Enlightenment on the French Revolution is one of the most important problems that confront the pure historian as well as the historian of thought and of literature. It is without doubt the most complex of the thousand aspects involved in the study of the Revolution. See Henri Peyre, "The Influence of Eighteenth-Century Ideas on the French Revolution" *Journal of the History* of Ideas, Vol. 10, No. 1 (Jan., 1949), pp. 63-87.

equality and popular democracy. Like the sans-culottes, many who aided the Republic of Spain advocated the abolition of the traditional authority and privileges of the monarchy, nobility, and Roman Catholic clergy.[145]

The Spanish War, which pitted an emerging bourgeois class, tenuously allied with a peasantry, against the Church and military, was a class war every bit as much as was the French Revolution. The backbone of the resistance against Franco's nationalist forces was comprised primarily of those with the greatest to gain through social and economic revolution -- the working class, especially urban trade unions whose political power grew the more Spain industrialized. It is, as George Orwell noted, "important to remember the working class remains the most reliable enemy of

---

[145] The sans-culottes, most of them peasants and urban laborers, served as the driving popular force behind the revolution. Though ill clad and ill equipped, they also made up the bulk of the Revolutionary army during the early years of the French Revolutionary Wars. Throughout the revolution, the sans-culottes provided the principal support behind the more radical and anti-bourgeoisie factions of the Paris Commune. The sans-culottes also populated the ranks of paramilitary forces charged with physically enforcing the policies and legislation of the revolutionary government, a task that not uncommonly included violence and the carrying out of executions against perceived enemies of the revolution. During the peak of their influence, the sans-culottes were seen as the truest and most authentic sons and daughters of the French Revolution, held up as living representations of the revolutionary spirit. During the height of revolutionary fervor, such as during the Reign of Terror when it was dangerous to be associated with anything counter-revolutionary, even public functionaries and officials actually from middle or upper-class backgrounds adopted the clothing and label of the sans-culottes as a demonstration of solidarity with the working class and patriotism for the new French Republic.

fascism (and monarchy), simply because the working-class stands to gain most by a decent reconstruction of society."[146] Sid Kaufman, an American volunteer, likewise noted that, "in all wars the proletariat suffers the greatest losses – they supply the largest part of the army, living standards go down, working class organizations are destroyed by patriotic pleas to aid the government in her hour of need, and the labor movement most always gets set back a while."[147]

But there are also some distinct differences between the French and American Revolutions and the Spanish War. For one, the Spanish War was a bit more industrial and global in scope than the French and American Revolutions, in large part because, by the 1930s, industrialization, as well as the proliferation of Enlightenment era discourse, had helped more widely spread class-consciousness around the globe than during the eighteenth century. Industrialization in particular, was increasingly dictating where people, such as peasants from Eastern European hinterlands lured to North and South America at the turn of the twentieth century, could find livelihoods.[148] The more

---

[146] George Orwell, "Looking back on the Spanish War" (London, New Road, 1943).

[147] Sidney Kaufman, September 12, 1938, Valencia, Spain, in Cary Nelson and Jefferson Hicks, eds. *Madrid 1937: Letters of the Abraham Lincoln Brigade From the Spanish Civil War* (New York, Routledge, 1996) 330.

[148] In Eric Hobsbawm's, *Primitive Rebels: Studies in Archaic Forms of Social Movement in the 19th and 20th Centuries*, the sans-culottes are perceived to be a transitional social group, midway between his "primitive rebels" (Lazzaretti, Andalusian Anarchists, Sicilian Fasci) and the modern working class. Speaking of those social groups, who must

people were forced from their ancestral homelands in search of steady work, the more widely ideas were circulated and exchanged.

But even the differences in centrality of agrarianism contrasted to industrialization that separated the revolutions of the eighteenth century, compared to the industrialization of the twentieth century, point to broad commonalities in revolutions. The American, French and Russian Revolutions, and the Spanish Republic were all largely inspired by centuries of oppression of workers by landed aristocracies, resulting in uprisings and sometimes actual revolts, with the goal of securing ownership of the land they worked, and subsequently political rights associated with owning land, as the primary objectives.

The cultural and social continuity between the French Revolution of 1789 and the rise of the Spanish

---

adapt to a modern capitalist economy or disappear, Hobsbawm says, "they come into it (the world of capitalism) as first-generation immigrants, or what is even more catastrophic, it comes to them from outside, insidiously by the operation of economic forces which they do not understand and over which they have no control, or brazenly by conquest, revolutions and fundamental changes of law whose consequences they do not understand, even when they have helped to bring them about. But due to a century and a half of industrialization and the circulation of Enlightenment Era ideas, many of the revolutionaries in Spain had a profound understanding of their role in the world and within the capitalist system. For more on industrialization and capitalism in shaping revolutions and revolutionaries see Hobsbawm's, *Primitive Rebels: Studies in Archaic Forms of Social Movement in the 19th and 20th Centuries* (New York, Norton, 1965) 3. Also see Bruce Mazlish, "The French Revolution in Comparative Perspective" *Political Science Quarterly*, Vol. 85, No. 2 (Jun., 1970), pp. 240-258.

Republic is especially pronounced. In both cases, Enlightenment Era-philosophy desacralized the authority of the King and the Church, and promoted a new society based on "reason" rather than tradition and the emergence of an influential bourgeoisie, which was formally part of the Third Estate (i.e. commoners) but had evolved into a caste with its own political agendas and aspired to social equality with aristocracy.[149] Such was the case in Spain, Russia, and the Americas as a result of class distinctions associated with industrialization during the nineteenth and twentieth centuries.[150]

One can especially see the influence of the French and Russian Revolutions during the Spanish War when considering the centrality of the commissar in the International Brigades. Carl Geiser explained the function of the commissar to his friend "Impy" in a letter home from Spain:

---

[149] A growing number of the French citizenry had absorbed the ideas of "equality" and "freedom of the individual" as presented by Voltaire, Jean-Jacques Rousseau, Denis Diderot and other philosophers and social theorists of the Enlightenment.

[150] One of the greatest continuities between the Russian Revolution and the rise of the Spanish Republic is rooted in industrialization. The rapid industrialization of Russia also resulted in urban overcrowding and poor conditions for urban industrial workers (as mentioned above). Between 1890 and 1910, the population of the capital, Saint Petersburg, swelled from 1,033,600 to 1,905,600, with Moscow experiencing similar growth. This created a new 'proletariat', which, due to being crowded together in the cities, was much more likely to protest and go on strike than the peasantry had been in previous decades.

The role of commissar originated in the Paris Commune, where the commune assigned trusted political workers to each military leader or commander who was trained in the old order, to control and guide his actions. It was necessary to use these military men because the new class did not have able and well-trained military leaders. The same was true in Russia in 1917, and also here in Spain where the political parties and trade unions appointed special delegates responsible politically, for the work of the early columns.[151]

Geiser often alluded to the War in Spain in terms of it being a revolution. "The government of the People's Front," he wrote his wife, consisted of "an alliance of all those who oppose fascism and national enslavement, of all who want a free and democratic Spain. The task of the revolution today is to deepen this alliance in the administration of the country for the victorious ending of the war, and for strengthening the economic and political power of the new type of democratic, republican parliamentary government."[152]

Geiser, who was a member of the Communist Party, had likely imbibed Karl Marx's *Eighteenth*

---

[151] Carl Geiser, Feb. 21, 1938, in Cary Nelson and Jefferson Hicks, eds. *Madrid 1937: Letters of the Abraham Lincoln Brigade From the Spanish Civil War* (New York, Routledge, 1996).

[152] Carl Geiser Papers, ALBA.004, Folder: Outgoing Correspondence, February 1938. Letter dated February 9, 1938. Tamiment Library/Robert F. Wagner Labor Archives. Elmer Holmes Tamiment Library, 70 Washington Square South, New York NY 10012, New York University Libraries.

Brumaire. Marx wrote, "The revolution is thoroughgoing. It is still traveling through purgatory. It does its work methodically." Spain in the 1930s was, volunteers such as Geiser believed, another stage in the series of revolutions leading to a break in history in which workers rather than employers would enjoy the balance of economic and political power, which Marx prophesized.

The American, French and Russian Revolutions all pitted economic and social elites with a monopoly of power against largely powerless workers (except the power and politics of violence), followed by counter-revolutions sponsored by national elites.[153] Such was the case in Spain: poor workers together with a rather skittish and reluctant bourgeois allies toppled a monarchy, only to face a counter-revolution by economic and social elites (namely the Catholic Church and moribund military).

---

[153] For more on oppressed people finding power through collective violence see Carl Leiden and Karl M. Schmitt, *The Politics of Violence: Revolution in the Modern World*) Prentice-Hall: Englewood Cliffs, N.J., 1968). Also see Hannah Arendt's essay *On Violence* distinguishes between violence and power. She maintains that, although theorists of both the Left and Right regard violence as an extreme manifestation of power, the two concepts are, in fact, antithetical. Power comes from the collective will and does not need violence to achieve any of its goals, since voluntary compliance takes its place. As governments start losing their legitimacy, violence becomes an artificial means toward the same end and is, therefore, found only in the absence of power. Bureaucracies then become the ideal birthplaces of violence since they are defined as the "rule by no one" against whom to argue and, therefore, recreate the missing links with the people they rule over. Hannah, Arendt, *On Violence*. Harvest Books (New York: Harcourt, Brace and World, 1970).

But the American volunteers' desire to fight fascism in Spain was more an immediate manifestation of liberal traditions in the American polity dating back to the second-half of the eighteenth century than the French and Russian Revolutions.[154] "The things he'll be fighting for with the Lincoln Battalion are the things, in one way, that I've fought for all my life – in a word, democracy, peace, security, freedom – the things they fought for in 1776," Fred Williams' father proudly boasted to a reporter for *The Southern Worker* in 1937.[155]

The American Revolution, like Spain's Popular Front Government, witnessed a popular uprising by a band that had subverted the power of the traditional aristocracy. Independence gave control to American radicals, who, imposing their advanced doctrines on a traditional society, transformed a rebellious secession into a social revolution. Such was the case in 1930s Spain. But the remnants of the earlier American aristocracy, though defeated, had not been eliminated. They were, like Franco's allies in Spain, able to reassert themselves. In the 1780's American conservatives gradually regained power until, in what amounted to a counter-revolution, they impressed their views indelibly on history in the new federal Constitution, in the revocation of some of the more enthusiastic actions of

---

[154] Allen Guttmann, *The Wound in the Heart: America and the Spanish Civil War* (New York, The Free Press/Macmillan, 1962).

[155] Pat Barr, "Mary and I are Glad Our Son Went to Spain: Southern Father and Mother Tell Us How the Spanish People's Fight For Democracy Belongs to Them" *Southern Worker: Magazine of the Common Worker of the South* Vol. V, No. 16. Chattanooga, Tenn. July 1937, 9.

the earlier revolutionary period, and in the Hamiltonian program for the new government. Politics in America, as in 1930s Spain, could be seen to have been a dialectical process in which an aristocracy of wealth and power struggled with the proverbial "People," who, ordinarily ill-organized and inarticulate, rose upon provocation, armed with powerful institutional and ideological weapons, to reform a corrupt and oppressive polity. Such was the case in 1930s Spain.

In all of this the underlying assumption is the belief that Enlightenment thought – the reforming ideas of advanced thinkers in eighteenth-century England and on the Continent – had been the effective lever by which American, French, Russian and Spanish radicals had turned a dispute over imperial relations into a sweeping reformation of public institutions and thereby laid the basis for politics and economics in each nation. But in each case, revolution was followed by counter-revolution. In many cases political revolutions led to worse economic and social situations than the climate that inspired revolutions in the first place. Such was the case in 1930s Spain.

The romantic themes central to the Enlightenment, and American and French Revolutions -- natural rights, religious liberty, liberal religion, free thought, universal progress and education – were also central to the Russian Revolution, which significantly influenced the war in Spain, especially the Anarchist-led social revolution between Trotskyists and Stalinists.[156]

---

[156] It is a commonplace to view other revolutions in the perspective of the French Revolution. For example, both later scholars and the participants of 1917 have seen a causal connection and a similarity of development between the

But the Anarchist-led revolution in Spain is especially instructive in two profound ways: first, it demonstrated how far Josef Stalin had dragged Russia away from the revolution led by Lenin after World War I; second, the discourse of revolution central to the American volunteers' correspondence helped demonstrate that they were by no means in Spain to fight for Stalin or the Soviet Union.

The conservative coup led by Franco, not inconsequentially, coincided with a leftist revolution led by Spanish anarchist groups, such as the National Confederation of Labor and Iberian Anarchist Federation (CNT-FAI). The Anarchists and the Workers' Party of Marxist Unification (POUM) were integrated into the Republican Army, but with stiff internal resistance from the Anarchists, who wanted no allegiance to the Communists; the POUM was later outlawed by the Communist Party and, like Trotskyists in general, falsely denounced as allies of Franco's fascist forces.

The Spanish Revolution was a workers' social revolution that began during the outbreak of the Spanish War in 1936 and resulted in the widespread implementation of anarchist and more broadly libertarian socialist organizational principles throughout various portions of the country for two to three years, primarily in Catalonia, Aragon, Andalusia, and parts of Valencia. Much of Spain's economy was put under worker control in anarchist strongholds like Catalonia,

---

French and the Russian Revolutions. See Bruce Mazlish, "The French Revolution in Comparative Perspective" *Political Science Quarterly*, Vol. 85, No. 2 (Jun., 1970), pp. 240-258.

where the figure was as high as seventy-five percent. Anarchist influence was, however, lower in areas such as Madrid where there was a heavier Communist Party influence. Factories in anarchist strongholds were run through worker committees, and agrarian areas became collectivized and run as libertarian communes. Even places like hotels, barbershops, and restaurants were collectivized and managed by their workers. The economic policies of the anarchist collectives were primarily operated according to the basic communist principle of "From each according to his ability, to each according to his need." In some places, money was abolished entirely and replaced with vouchers and coupons distributed on the basis of need rather than individual labor contributions. The agrarian collectives had considerable success despite opposition and lack of resources.

   This revolution was opposed by both the Soviet-supported communists, who ultimately took their orders from Stalin's politburo (which feared a loss of political control and the requisite discipline necessary to win a war), and the Social Democratic Republicans (who worried about the loss of civil property rights). As the war dragged on, the spirit of the revolutions' early days waned in large part due to demonization on behalf of the Soviet Union – the Republic's reluctant ally.

   Comintern policy was that the war was not the time for the revolution because wars cannot be won without order and discipline, and that, until total victory had been won, there could be no social revolution in Spain. The primary goal in the Spanish War, Stalin believed, had to be the defeat of the Nationalists, not the abolition of capitalism. In 2007 Eric Hobsbawm justified the Soviet reaction to the anarchist revolution in an editorial published in *The Guardian*:

A serious war conducted by a government requires structure, discipline and a degree of centralization. What characterizes social revolutions like that of 1936 is local initiative, spontaneity, independence of, or even resistance to, higher authority – this was especially so given the unique strength of anarchism in Spain... The conflict between libertarian enthusiasm and disciplined organization, between social revolution and winning a war, remains real in the Spanish Civil War, even if we suppose that the USSR and the Communist Party wanted the war to end in revolution and that the parts of the economy socialized by the anarchists (i.e. handed over to local workers' control) worked well enough. Wars, however flexible the chains of command, cannot be fought, or war economies run, in a libertarian fashion. The Spanish Civil War could not have been waged, let alone won, along Orwellian lines.[157]

Many other left-wing parties, particularly the anarchists and POUM, who George Orwell fought amongst during the Spanish War, vehemently disagreed with the Soviet Party line; to them, and many American volunteers, the war and the revolution were one and the same.[158] In this

---

[157] Eric Hobsbawm, "War of Ideas," *The Guardian*, 2/17/2007.

[158] Thomas, *The Spanish Civil War*, (New York, Random House, 2001) 683. Despite the critics clamoring for "maximum efficiency" rather than revolutionary methods, anarchist collectives often produced more than before the collectivization. In Aragon, for instance, the productivity increased by 20%. The idea of "free love" became widely

sense, the Soviet Union was a counter-revolutionary force whose main goal was a political ally and bulwark against Germany; not the death of capitalism or fascism in Spain.

Alexander Orlov, the chief of the People's Commissariat for Internal Affairs (NKVD) went to Spain at the end of August, 1936 with the major task of purging POUM. On December 17, 1936 *Pravada*, Soviet Russia's most prominent ideological organ, wrote that in Catalonia "the cleaning up of the Trotskyist and Anarcho-Syndicalist elements … will be carried out with the same energy as in the USSR" (i.e. with murder and political prisons). A few days later the Comintern executive wrote to the Spanish Communist Party that "whatever happens, the final destruction of the Trotskyists must be achieved."[159]

The inauguration of the Popular Front in Spain in 1936, ironically, caused a shift in Communist Party dogma, diverging significantly from the discourse of revolution that marked the Russian Revolution that began in 1917, which was heavily influenced by Karl Marx, whose work was especially informed by the French Revolution. The Soviet Union's support of a centrist, non-communist, non-socialist Republican Spanish government demonstrated that Stalin was himself a fascist dictator dedicated to maintaining the political and social status quo inside Russia above all

---

prevalent. In many ways, this spirit of cultural liberation prefigured that of the "New Left" movements of the 1960s.

[159] Michael Alpert, *A New International History of the Spanish Civil War* (New York, Palgrave Macmillan, 1994) 146.

else.[160] The presence of Soviet military advisors and Soviet-built equipment, many of which were antiques acquired from museums, nevertheless increased the prestige and power of the Spanish Communist Party, enabling Stalinist agents to throttle rival anarchist and social revolutionary parties in Catalonia, ultimately crushing the revolution and tragically aiding Franco's regime, which survived until 1975.

Nevertheless, the American volunteers' sense of idealism was especially rooted in a profound sympathy for the Spanish people, and ultimately more consonant with the Anarchists of Spain than for the Soviets, thereby complicating conservative critics' assertions that Americans were fighting to advance Bolshevism.

American volunteers' letters consistently expressed solidarity with and affection for the worker, the intellectual, the peasant for those who had deposed the centuries old monarchy, instituted land reforms, built schools, and brought to the Spanish Cortes a program of government that could bridge the gap between the remnants of feudalism and industrialization and the benefits of an enlightened democracy.[161] Many letters especially evoke revolutionary discourse rooted in the dialectics of the Enlightenment. Americans who went to Spain were thus ultimately impelled by the domestic and international crises of the 1930s to defend

---

[160] Ann Talbot, "Eric Hobsbawm on the Spanish Civil War: an anti-historical tirade," 16 March 2007, World Socialist Website.

[161] Arthur H. Landis, *The Abraham Lincoln Brigade* (New York, Citadel Press, 1967).

what, to very many of them, seemed to be the "cause of western civilization itself," especially a defense of liberty, equality, fraternity and democracy, which many were convinced was imperiled by Franco, Hitler, and Mussolini.[162]

---

[162] Robert A. Rosenstone, "The Men of the Abraham Lincoln Battalion," *The Journal of American History*, Vol. 54, No. 2 (Sep., 1967), pp. 327-338.

Chapter Five

"Volunteers for Liberty"

The Lincoln Battalion newsletter was originally called *The Volunteer For Liberty*. The title helps underscore the central reason many American volunteers believed they were fighting in Spain – for liberty. A Columbia trained physician, Edward Barsky, who volunteered, said that in Spain they wanted "only liberty" to "think each according to his conscience, not to starve in fertile fields untilled, to live un-menaced by secret police." This "modest liberty, this democracy which the Spaniard had legally won at the polls without civil war, seemed as valuable to me as it did to them."[163] Fascism, many American volunteers believed, was the antithesis of the liberty expressed in Enlightenment Era discourse. One of the most prominent themes elaborated in volunteers' letters home to friends and family regarding why they believed they were fighting fascists in Spain was rooted in the language of liberty, which was especially manifest in demands for progress, democracy, and freedom of religion. Religious freedom, or at least lack of oppression by the Church, was ultimately consonant with democratic/anti-monarchial principles central to the Enlightenment, French Revolution, Russian Revolution, and the war in Spain. The Republic's political influence superseded the monarchy in 1931.

Though political power had shifted from right to center, economic power had not changed much, and

---

[163] Edward Barsky in Peter N. Carroll & James D. Fernadez, *Facing Fascism: New York & The Spanish Civil War* (New York, NYU Press, 2007) 56.

those holding that power soon united with the Church and Army against the democratically elected government. By 1933, there was twelve percent unemployment throughout Spain; in the southern, less industrialized part of the country, that figure was nearly twenty percent. Deprivation was, in short, widespread. As bad as the Great Depression was for the American poor and working class, it was even more excruciating for Spain's peasantry, where there was nothing akin to the New Deal designed to alleviate the suffering of the poor.

Despite some modest centrist sponsored reforms, Spain's economy was, like everywhere in the world, in shambles and the 1933 elections witnessed a stark shift to the right as a result of economic depression together with elites using their political and economic power to wrest power back from the centrists. As was the case in the Depression Era United States, wages in Spain were cut sharply, many jobs were eliminated altogether, rents were raised, and tenants were summarily evicted in both cities and the hinterland. Like all revolutions in human history up to the 1930s, the war in Spain centered on the distribution of land and the social privileges and liberties associated with land ownership. Many landowners, meanwhile, let their land holdings go idle, which resulted in their farm tenants being without a livelihood.[164] This created a starving force of people desperate for some kind of social revolution.

---

[164] Hank Rubin, foreword by Peter N. Carroll, *Spain's Cause Was Mine: A Memoir of an American Medic in the Spanish Civil War* (Carbondale, Southern Illinois University Press, 1997) 20.

American volunteer William Sennett wrote a friend named "Gussie" in June, 1937 explaining the centrality of land and class in his decision to fight for the Republic:

> I never realized the extent of the importance of the peasant question as I see most clearly now. Even in Madrid we see the mules and ox carts of the Spanish peasants. Their entire existence is based on the soil. The majority of the Spanish people (58%) depend on the development of the land for their livelihood. Previous to the Popular Front Government most of the land belonged to rich dukes and lords who hired peasant labor at exorbitantly low wages, from 1 and a half to five pesetas a day. The vast lands, covering tens of thousands of acres, were in the main uncultivated due to primitive methods. The peasants were kept in ignorance, could neither read nor write. The development of the Popular Front movement shows the leading role of the workers in the class struggle… It was the workers who formed their trade union organizations and political parties who succeeded in bringing about popular reforms that even bettered the position of the peasantry… The Popular Front Government in existence since February, 1936 has given the land to the peasants. It is true the type of distribution is varied but in one form or another the land is in the hands of the people who till the soil.[165]

---

[165] William Sennett June 3, 1937, Albacete, Spain, in Cary Nelson and Jefferson Hicks, eds. *Madrid 1937: Letters of the*

The Popular Front's victory in the winter of 1936 that Sennett alluded to touched off a whole series of events: the government granted amnesty to political prisoners jailed during the dictatorship that lasted from 1933 to 1936 and a series of agrarian reforms settled between 50,000 – 100,000 peasants on their own land before the end of March; employers who had laid off employees had to hire them back and indemnify them for lost wages. At the same time, however, the value of the peseta fell sharply, and leading financiers began to send their wealth out of the country to places such as the U.S. and Switzerland.[166] All this helped trigger the coup by Franco's anti-democratic fascist forces, who were ardently supported by the Church's hierarchy and monarchists.

This rapid shifting within the Spanish government from left to right, together with reforms, followed quickly by the unraveling of reform measures, served as fodder for American volunteers' letters. Many of them saw the fascists as antipodal to the progressivism they had fought for on picket lines in the U.S. and battlefronts of Spain.

The language of progress and egalitarianism in contrast to social regression and repression was especially prominent in American volunteers' correspondence all throughout the war, but especially in

---

Abraham Lincoln Brigade From the Spanish Civil War (New York, Routledge, 1996) 311-312.

[166] Hank Rubin, foreword by Peter N. Carroll, *Spain's Cause Was Mine: A Memoir of an American Medic in the Spanish Civil War* (Carbondale, Southern Illinois University Press, 1997) 21.

the latter stages when things were going very badly for the Republic. Sidney Rosenblatt, for instance, urged his friend, Estelle to "use your progressive education for the progressive education of others."[167] Seven months later he explained, "Everything that is happening is clear and understandable," he wrote. "It's a fight against barbarism and fascism – for peace and progress and a happy life for all time."[168]

In the minds of many American volunteers, fascism represented total regression of humanity, an industrialized reversion to monarchial rule and subsequent peasantry of workers all over the world. "The power of Spain's royal family (which backed Franco's fascists) offended my sense of democracy and fairness," American volunteer Hank Rubin wrote.[169] To

---

[167] Sidney Rosenblatt to Estelle, June 10, 1937; Rosenblatt Papers, ALBA.261, Folder: "outgoing correspondence; Tamiment Library/Robert F. Wagner Labor Archives. Elmer Holmes Tamiment Library, 70 Washington Square South, New York NY 10012, New York University Libraries. Rosenblatt and Estelle were both members of the YCL. Rosenblatt was a native New Yorker who attend the City College of New York. He sailed for Franceaboard the *Statendam* and arrived in Spain, June 24, 1937. He was captured by Nationalists March 10, 1938 in Belchite while attending to the mortally wounded David Reiss. He was exchanged April 22, 1939, and returned to the U.S. May 6, 1939 aboard the *President Harding*.

[168] Sidney Rosenblatt to Estelle, January 20, 1938; Rosenblatt Papers, ALBA.261, Folder: "outgoing correspondence; Tamiment Library/Robert F. Wagner Labor Archives. Elmer Holmes Tamiment Library, 70 Washington Square South, New York NY 10012, New York University Libraries.

[169] Hank Rubin, foreword by Peter N. Carroll, *Spain's Cause Was Mine: A Memoir of an American Medic in the Spanish*

many volunteers, liberty was synonymous with progress and fascism was one-in-the-same as oppression. In 1937 Canute Frankson likewise wrote that:

> We, who have identified ourselves with the progressive elements, have learned that our enemies are not the whites as such, but an international band of monied overlords. They have taken up arms and are mercilessly slaughtering men, women and children of their own race. These wolves can fool us no longer. We have taken off the sheep's clothing. We felt that it was really a question of the salvation of democracy, of liberty, of life and civilization. And because we knew these things, we left home, and all, to stake our lives on the side of the progressive elements. That is why I'm here. This same fascism which invaded Ethiopia and subdued some of its people is the same fascism we fight here in Spain. It is the same fascism which re-action [sic] would force on the people of America... The world is now passing through a painful and very critical period. The rulers of some countries have organized themselves into a vicious band, determined to deprive the people of all their civil liberties and enslave them for further exploitation and oppression. In Germany, Italy and Japan this is already an accomplished fact. Under their pretense of "national salvation" the dictators of these countries have destroyed the people's culture, dissolved their organizations and trade unions,

---

Civil War (Carbondale, Southern Illinois University Press, 1997) 19.

imprisoned, tortured and murdered their leaders, and have made their countries a living hell under the despotic heels of militarism. All policies affecting the people are dictated from the all-powerful head who holds the penalty of death over the heads of those who may dare question such authority… it is very evident here that they are out to destroy everything which represents progress."[170]

The notion that fascism was the antithesis of progress and reason was nearly pervasive amongst the volunteers, at least those whose letters were preserved. "I cannot see any basis for anyone failing to support the Spanish people who has the slightest regard for democracy and all that it implies of possibility for education, progress and development, all of which was stifled under the old regime," volunteer Sheldon Jones surmised in a March 1938 letter. "It seems to me also that a curb must be put up against Nazi aggression and Mussolini's Blackshirts unless the world is to be thrown back into the dark ages."[171] In his 1939 memoir of his experience fighting fascists in Spain, Alvah Bessie expressed a similar sentiment regarding the Republic's enemies, and the lack of freedom and subsequent,

---

[170] Canute Frankson to friend, Steve Nelson Box 1, Folder, Canute Frankson, Letters From Spain. Tamiment Library/Robert F. Wagner Labor Archives. Elmer Holmes Tamiment Library, 70 Washington Square South, New York NY 10012, New York University Libraries.

[171] Sheldon Jones, March 8, 1938, in Marcel Acier, ed, *From Spanish Trenches: Recent Letters From Spain* (New York, Modern Age, 1937), 146. Jones arrived in France on Valentine's Day, 1937 aboard the *S.S. Paris* and returned February 4, 1939 aboard the *President Harding*.

perceived reigning in of social progress he believed they represented: "The class upon which the monarchy had rested, the owning class and those whose interests tied in with the interests of the owning class," he wrote. "Every mild reform that the Republic attempted was opposed and sabotaged by these people, who fell into four groups: the landlords, the industrialists, the Spanish Catholic hierarchy and the Army."[172]

---

[172]Alvah Bessie, *Men in Battle: A Story of Americans in Spain*, (New York, Scribner, 1939), 346. *Alvah Bessie* was born in New York City on June 4, 1904 to Daniel Nathan Cohen Bessie, a successful businessman and inventor, and Adeline Schlesinger. The younger of two boys, Bessie was raised in ease in the then-prosperous precincts of Harlem. He attended public school, graduated from Dewitt Clinton High School and, in 1920, enrolled in Columbia University. Bessie's rebellious nature often placed him at odds with his father's conservative values and authoritarian manner. When, in 1922, Daniel Bessie died after suffering a severe economic setback, he left his family in a precarious financial state, but Alvah Bessie free to pursue his own ambitions. Bessie completed his degree and graduated from Columbia in 1924 with a B.A. in English. Through a friend, he found work as an actor with Eugene O'Neill's Provincetown Players. For the next four years Bessie immersed himself in the New York theater scene, performing with the Provincetown Players, the Theater Guild and with actor-manager Walter Hampden's repertory company in a production of Cyrano de Bergerac. Recognizing his limited talent as an actor, he left the theater and, in 1928, traveled to France to join the community of American expatriates in Paris intent on becoming a writer. During his brief stay in France, he worked as a rewrite man at the Paris-Times, and wrote "Redbird," his first short story to receive publication. He returned to New York in 1929, and for the next six years, his stories, essays, and reviews appeared in *The New Republic, Scribner, Atlantic Monthly, Saturday Review of Literature, Collier's* and *Story*. In July 1930, he married Mary Burnett, a puppet-maker and artist. The couple moved to Vermont and had two boys -- Daniel and David. Bessie began work on his first novel, Dwell in the Wilderness. During this

time, Bessie also began to study Marxist theory and question his political convictions. Bessie was awarded a Guggenheim Fellowship following the publication of his novel in 1935, and, with his family, returned to New York. Back in the City, Bessie began to move in more radical circles, and in 1936 he became a member of the Communist Party. In 1935 he joined the staff of the *Brooklyn Daily Eagle*, serving as drama and book editor. His tenure at the paper was marked by dissent. His radical stance on striking maritime workers in 1936 and on the Spanish Civil War ran counter to management's more conservative views. A final dispute with the paper stemmed from his praise of French novelist and aviator Andre Malraux's efforts to organize a squadron of French flyers to aid the Spanish Republic. In 1937 he resigned from the *Eagle* and went to work in the public relations office of the Spanish Information Bureau, a New York agency of the Republican Government. During this period, the Bessies' marriage began to founder. The couple separated and soon after divorced. On January 22, 1938, Bessie sailed to Spain on the S.S. Lafayette to join the International Brigade's fight against the Franco-led rebellion. Although he earned his pilot's license before leaving for Spain with the objective of serving as a flyer, he was assigned to a front-line combat unit with the Abraham Lincoln Brigade, participating in the Ebro offensive from July to September 1938, and attaining the rank of sergeant-adjutant. He also served as a correspondent for the International Brigade's publication The Volunteer for Liberty. He daily chronicled his personal experiences in a series of notebooks, and upon his return to the United States, these jottings became the basis of his wartime memoirs, *Men in Battle* (1939). From 1939 to 1943, Bessie was film and theatre critic for the New Masses, and, under a pseudonym, wrote a regular column for a Young Communist League publication. He remained active in the Spanish Republican cause, working on behalf of the Joint Anti-Fascist Refugee Committee writing articles and delivering speeches. He started writing screenplays and moved to California in 1943 when Warner Brothers studios hired him as a contract writer. During World War II, he served as Second Lieutenant in the Civil Air Patrol, Los Angeles Squadron 3. In 1945 his original story that was the basis for the screenplay of "Objective Burma" was nominated for an Academy Award. His other screen credits from this time include, "Hotel Berlin," "The Very Thought of You," "Northern Pursuit, " and "Smart Woman." He was fired from Warner

One of the most glaring signs of social regression in Spain, many American volunteers believed, was the power of the Catholic Church, whose sway was comparable to the Catholic Church in France prior to their first revolution.

Brothers in 1945 in the wake of his outspoken support of striking studio workers. In September 1947, the House Un-American Activities Committee (HUAC) launched an investigation on the influence of the Communist Party in the motion-picture industry. Over fifty people were called to testify and answer questions regarding political affiliations and associations. Bessie, along with nine other Hollywood figures, refused to comply with the Committee's demands. They were cited for contempt of Congress, given one-year prison sentences, and became known as the "Hollywood Ten." Bessie served out his term in a federal correctional facility in Texarkana, Texas and was blacklisted in Hollywood. After his release from prison, Bessie relocated to San Francisco and found employment with the International Longshoremen's and Warehouseman's Union as editor of The Dispatcher, the union newspaper. In 1951 he edited, The Heart of Spain, an anthology of writings on the Spanish Civil War published and distributed by the Veterans of the Abraham Lincoln Brigade. Throughout the 60s and 70s, Bessie worked as a publicist for San Francisco arts organizations including the San Francisco Mime Troupe and the San Francisco Film Festival. He also worked as stage manager and lighting technician for the hungry i nightclub, an experience that inspired the novel, One for My Baby (1980). He married Sylviane Muller in 1963. (Muller was his third wife; his second marriage, to Helen Clare Nelson, ended in divorce). In 1968, Bessie collaborated on the Spanish film, *Espana otra vez*, and offered an account of the production and his return to Spain in his memoir Spain Again. He remained active in the Bay Area chapter of the Veterans of the Abraham Lincoln Brigade, and in 1975, he was honored at the 39th Anniversary Dinner. Before he could complete work on Our Fight, a VALB anthology devoted to the writings of Lincoln Brigade veterans, Bessie died of a heart attack on July 21, 1985. He was 81 years old. Biography courtesy of Tamiment Library, NYU.

The Catholic Church in 1930s Spain was, like the Church in 1790s France, a moribund corporation. But the Church in Spain's tyranny was perhaps even more egregious as a result of industrialization: it owned enormous tracts of land, as well as factories, power plants, hotels, department stores and newspapers, all of which strengthened the institution's political power by making peasants especially dependent on the Clergy for survival.

For hundreds of years the Church and monarchy in Spain worked in tandem to maintain a rigid social hierarchy in which the Clergy were powerful landowners and thus entitled to special economic and political privileges. Every priest in Spain had been on the public payroll prior to the rise of the Second Republic. Spain's government had been a centuries-old oligarchy controlled by rich and powerful landowners, caudillos and the Clergy, to quite abruptly being a democratic republic of the moderate left loosely held together by tenuous alliances of the most reformist section of the organized working class, along with socialists, the petty bourgeoisie, and some reluctant Republicans – all ideologically united against the Ancient Regime's monopoly on political power. The Popular Front Republican government had the temerity to strip the Church of some of its longtime political privileges, arguing that the institution had too much secular power, and reduced some of its subsidiaries. The Church's economic interests, in short, largely influenced its political alliance with Franco's fascists.

For the first time in Spain's history, following the 1936 election, religious freedom was made national policy. State financial support for the Clergy and religious orders were eliminated almost overnight, and the religious hierarchy was quickly stripped of its secular power. Orders such as the Jesuits, which had a long-held allegiance to the Vatican, were dissolved. The Republic had divorced church and state and settled tenant farmers, accustomed to beseeching clergy for the most basic human services, on great estates whose owners often lived in the lap of luxury on the French Riviera, while their peasantry worked for a hand-to-mouth subsistence on land they could never own. The republic that rose in 1930s Spain also wrested public education from the Church and placed it into the hands of the state. Despite compulsory Catholic indoctrination into the 1930s, between fifty-five to seventy percent of the country's population was illiterate, wholly dependent on clergymen for deciphering meaning of scripture, law and order.[173] When "the sway of Catholicism" over "education was broken," William Sennett wrote to a friend in June of 1937, "the people of Spain were sweeping away feudal survivals."[174]

---

[173] Cary Nelson and Jefferson Hicks, eds. *Madrid 1937: Letters of the Abraham Lincoln Brigade From the Spanish Civil War* (New York, Routledge, 1996), 311.

[174] William Sennett, June 3, 1937, Albacete, Spain, in Cary Nelson and Jefferson Hicks, eds. *Madrid 1937: Letters of the Abraham Lincoln Brigade From the Spanish Civil War* (New York, Routledge, 1996) 312. The story of Sennett's life from Communist functionary to corporate executive is told in detail in his oral history on file in the Bancroft Library at the University of California at Berkeley. Born in Chicago of Russian immigrant parents, Sennett's early life was one of poverty. His first language was Yiddish, but he quickly learned English in Chicago grammar schools. Growing up during the Great Depression, he developed a lifelong dedication to the needs of poor people. Although his formal schooling stopped at ninth grade, he was well-read, and had a

lifelong passion for learning. As a youth he was outraged when he saw families who couldn't pay rent forced from their homes, the doors padlocked, and their furniture moved onto the sidewalk. He discovered that the Communist Party had a strategy to help them. Young Communists would break the pad-locks and move the furniture back into the houses before the police arrived. Under the law the landlord had to go back to court and file for another eviction notice. In the interim, the Communists would get the tenants on welfare. Impressed, Sennett joined the Young Communist League, and later the Communist Party. In 1937 he volunteered to go to Spain to fight in the International Brigades. He arrived just as the Republic received new trucks, and was assigned as a driver. For the remainder of the war he worked in transportation, moving supplies to the front. After Spain, Sennett married, had a child, and went to work in the defense industry. This gave him a draft deferment. But he volunteered for military service in 1943 and was assigned to the Army Air Corps at Keesler Field, Mississippi. He was slated for advanced training when the FBI advised his commanding officer of his Communist background. He was then put in charge of teaching illiterates reading, writing and mathematics. After the war, the McCarran Act ushered in a period of repression of Communists, and Sennett went underground. He was already becoming disillusioned with Communism when Khrushchev made his famous anti-Stalin speech in 1956. Sennett left the party, and sought a new life. He found it in the transportation industry. His administrative and negotiating skills led him to a job with the Strick company, at that time a part of Fruehauf Corporation. The company manufactured and leased truck trailers for heavy freight. Through many company mergers, Sennett rose in the corporate hierarchy. Eventually he became the president of Transport International Pool (TIP). He built the company into a multimillion-dollar corporation headquartered in San Francisco with 66 branches nationwide and 26 in ten foreign countries. Convinced that socialism was possible if it was strictly democratic, he became publisher of the Chicago-based, left-leaning weekly *In These Times*. He also supported many organizations dedicated to the elimination of poverty and racism. He helped organize the San Francisco tenants' organizations and the passage of rent control legislation. He died of complications of Alzheimer's disease on March 30, 2003, in San Francisco at age 88.

The Republic's social reforms were nothing short of revolutionary in contrast to the centuries that preceded the 1930s, in which the Church and Monarchy had reigned supreme over a fledgling peasantry, who were a caste. Franco's coup was thus a kind of counter-revolution that received unqualified support from the Church hierarchy, the Army – which was, like the Clergy, also a privileged caste – and of the landlords who saw their privilege and political power slipping ever so slightly into the hands of the peasantry they had exploited for centuries. The Army and Church were also predominately supported by Spain's industrialists, who valued a pliant, docile, and easily manipulated and replaceable labor force.

But the conflation of Soviet-led organization of the International Brigades with what seemed to be an assault on the Catholic Church's traditional privilege and subsequent power helped win public support for the fascists in the United States and other western democracies, especially the followers of demagogues like Father Coughlin. Most of the Catholic backing for Franco came, apparently, from men and women who felt that the Spanish insurgents were fighting against communism and for a kind of Catholicism that was consonant with ideals loosely referred to as the "American Way of Life."[175] Even some close friends of American volunteers for the Republic, such as William Sennett, questioned the volunteers' motives after reading of churches burned and the killing of priests and

---

[175] Allen Guttmann, *The Wound in the Heart: America and the Spanish Civil War* (New York, The Free Press/Macmillan, 1962) 202.

nuns by Anarchists and Communists, which prompted the following spirited response:

> The Catholic Church previous to the war was an organic part of the state apparatus. It owned 1/3 of the land in Spain, controlled all education, and was the dominating influence in reactionary political life, which kept Spain from taking her place with the advanced countries of the world. When the coalition of progressive forces established the republic, similar to our own in America, it decreed the separation of church and state and took practical measures to give land to the peasantry. Thus, the Church was to continue as an institution, with the right to religious worship not solely confined to those of the Catholic faith. This is as we have it at home, but this is not as the upper hierarchy of the Church would have it. It is from this lust for economic and political power that certain officials of the Church conspired and gave their blessings to an armed uprising to overthrow a government legally constituted, which in the previous election had obtained a majority vote. Hitler, who is particularly vicious against the Catholic Church in Germany, peculiarly found it easy to collaborate with the Italian fascist dictator, Mussolini, in sending in whole armies of men and materials in the name of Christianity!... Priests who fought with the fascist murderers are treated as enemies of the people but you must also remember that there are many priests who have remained loyal (and I have seen them) and are fighting with gun in hand against those who betrayed the faith. There are hundreds of

nuns who are working with might and main amongst the loyalist soldiers helping to relieve the suffering at the front. I have visited churches in Madrid, Valencia, and Barcelona and have spoken with the heroic priests who administer the services under bomb and shell.[176]

There were, in fact, as Sennett's letter elaborated, many members of the Clergy sympathetic to the peasantry, as they had seen and understood firsthand the widespread suffering of their congregants. But the Catholic hierarchy's official policies were in support of Franco's fascists, who sought to restore the traditional (and arbitrary) power, privilege, and prestige of the Church and Monarchy, particularly the Carlists.

The Nationalists' official slogan of "God, Fatherland, King" sharply contrasted the language of liberty, equality, and fraternity pervasive in many American volunteers' correspondence.[177] But Spain was,

---

[176] William Sennett to Augusta, January 30, 1938, Albacete, Spain, in Cary Nelson and Jefferson Hicks, eds. *Madrid 1937: Letters of the Abraham Lincoln Brigade From the Spanish Civil War* (New York, Routledge, 1996) 319.

[177] It is important to note that Franco also tried to appropriate "fraternity, liberty, and egalitarian," which especially helps demonstrate the centrality of Enlightenment era discourse to the Spanish War. But his alliance with CEDA, a Christian paramilitary group in league with the Church as well as the fascist Falange Blueshirts, and Carlist monarchs helped center the right's slogans along conservative lines such as "God, Fatherland, King" as well as "family and corporation." Franco was, at the core of his being a military man and capitalist who believed thought dictatorship could "harmonize Spain." For more on the rightwing alliance see episode four of the documentary series, *The Spanish Civil War* (London, Granada Production/BBC, 1983).

much like the American Civil War, a brutal conflict that pitted brother against brother, and nun against nun. Many of the churches burned by Communists and Anarchists had been used as sanctuary for Nationalist troops, including Muslim Moors from Morocco, who were Nationalist mercenaries, as well as crack snipers who often used church bell towers as vantage points to kill loyalists and civilians.

In spite of red baiting by publications owned by the likes of William Randolph Hearst, even *Life Magazine*, which was by no means leftist in contrast to the *Daily Worker, New Masses* and others, published a feature article on the Lincoln Battalion with the title "Americans Have Died Fighting for Democracy in Spain." There was widespread belief amongst the volunteers and people back in the United States that they were not fighting for a left-wing regime, per se, but rather for the lawfully elected government of the Spanish Republic.[178] Lincoln vet Morris Stamm, a labor organizer from Cleveland, explained his reasons behind going to Spain by linking an inevitable imbalance of political power in a democracy with class inequity:

> Those who hide or conceal the class struggle in this country (the U.S.) are the middle-class intellectuals, managers of companies, or owners of middle-sized companies. Workers know about the class struggle… In Spain we went, I went, in order to allow or to help the Spanish people win their political independence… We didn't go to Spain to tell them that they had to

---

[178] Hugh M. Jenkins, "Free For All" The Washington Post, May 31, 1997, A.17.

follow a certain kind of politics, or to establish a certain kind of society or a certain kind of government. We went there to help them achieve the possibility of choosing.[179]

American volunteer Robert Munson Taylor likewise wrote a friend that:

If only the working class of these countries could see the situation in its right light. If they would only ignore the reactionary reports of Hearst and the other capitalist papers and read the true story of Spain. If they would only see in the true light what an easy job we anti-fascists would have, but as they don't we must work like hell until a true democracy is established throughout the world.[180]

---

[179] Morris Stamm in John Gerassi, *The Premature Antifascists: North American Volunteers in the Spanish Civil War 1936-39: An Oral History* (New York, Praeger, 1986) 78-79. Stamm was born September 22, 1904 in the Ukraine. He was a member of the YCL. He sailed for France aboard the *Rotterdam* and arrived in Spain May 5, 1937. He was wounded in action September 4, 1937 in Belchite, and returned to the U.S. aboard the *President Harding* one New Year's Eve, 1938.

[180] Robert Munson Taylor, April 20, 1937, in Marcel Acier, ed, *From Spanish Trenches: Recent Letters From Spain* (New York, Modern Age, 1937) 151. Born in Boston, Massachusetts, Robert Munson Taylor (1913-?) went to Spain in January 1937 to fight with the International Brigades in the Spanish Civil War as a member of the Abraham Lincoln Brigade. During his time in Spain, he suffered a head injury and was at one point mistakenly reported as dead. Taylor fought in several major battles, including those in Villanueva de la Canada and Brunete. He was living in Detroit during the summer of 1938 when the local Red Squad raided his house and held him for two days. He was accused of illegally recruiting volunteers for Spain, and a political file was kept on him for the next forty

A similar sentiment was expressed by Sennett in a letter to a friend from the Aragon Front in April 1938: "if the powers that believe in the democratic form of government were to band together now and undertake economic action against the bandit nations," he wrote, "they would check their war schemes and give impetus to the further development of democracy."[181]

Many, including the Communist Party of the United States, who had played a large role in organizing the International Brigades, saw the war in Spain as an extension of American democratic values. Bill Lawrence, in an article titled "Democracy's Stake in Spain," asserted that, "Names like Oliver Law, Harry Hines, Rudolf Tieger, Steve Nelson, Bob Merriman, Joe Dallet, and Milton Herndon and scores of others (that had died) will never be forgotten in the history of the struggle for democracy."[182] Henry Wileman who was hunkered down in a Spanish trench in March, 1937 likewise wrote a friend that, "the (Spanish) people are for democracy.

---

years. In 1940 he was again arrested, this time by the FBI, when crossing the Canadian border into Michigan. By 1990, Taylor (then living in Birmingham, Michigan) had succeeded in obtaining copies of his Detroit Red Squad files. Biography courtesy of Tamiment Library, NYU. The collection includes little information about Taylor's life following the war, but it is apparent that he regularly kept in touch with other Abraham Lincoln Brigade veterans.

[181] William Sennett, April 16, 1938, in Cary Nelson and Jefferson Hicks, eds. *Madrid 1937: Letters of the Abraham Lincoln Brigade From the Spanish Civil War* (New York, Routledge, 1996) 325.

[182] Earl Browder and Bill Lawrence, *Next Steps to Win the War in Spain*, "Democracy's Stake in Spain," (New York, Workers Library Publishers, January 1938) 20.

And to see a people in this transitory stage is something you can never forget, once you are a part of it."[183]

In other words, *The Volunteer For Liberty* as well as publications run by men as centrist and capitalist as Henry Luce, the man who later coined the phrase "American Century," as well as those who risked life, limb and citizenship for high-minded ideals rooted in Enlightenment discourse were all convinced that the fascism American volunteers were fighting represented the antithesis of the liberty that the United States supposedly valued so deeply. This is especially evident in American volunteers' correspondence, namely in their demands for progress and democracy, both of which were especially threatened by the alliance of monarchists, clergy and fascists in Spain and throughout the world.

---

[183] Henry Wileman, March 28, 1937, Murcia, Spain, Marcel Acier, ed, *From Spanish Trenches: Recent Letters From Spain* (New York, Modern Age, 1937) 154. Wileman was a construction worker and member of the CP while residing in New York City. He sailed for France aboard the *President Roosevelt*, and arrived in Spain July 21, 1937. He returned to the U.S aboard the *Ausonia*, December 20, 1938.

Chapter Six

"Volunteers for Equality"

American volunteers' letters home to friends and family indicate a deep concern for equality as well as liberty, both of which were, in many minds of those who volunteered to fight fascists in Spain, deeply connected. The volunteers' quest for social and economic equality is especially deduced in their demands for an end to the inequity associated with class and race. While their letters often evoked differences in their class, race, ethnicity, and politics, there is a great deal of continuity in regard to a universal stance against the threat of fascism in contrast to Enlightenment Era ideas associated with liberty, equality and fraternity. These ideals were, for many of the American volunteers, the primary impetus for risking life, limb and citizenship in the Spanish War.

Many of those who comprised the International Brigades, including the American volunteers, saw the war in Spain as an extension of inveterate class conflicts in their home countries. The protest movements of the tumultuous 1930s rested firmly on a historical bedrock of earlier political influences and causes such as American populism, labor protests, the creation of the Socialist Party, the formation of the Industrial Workers of the World, as well as Enlightenment Era discourse, and the American Revolution.

It is especially important to note the growing power of labor unions during and after the Progressive Era in emboldening workers on a scale never before or since seen in human history. John L. Lewis formed the Congress of Industrial Organizations in 1935, which in twenty months grew to more than three million members. New industrial unions in steel, auto, rubber, and the oil industries, organized on an unheard-of scale, and challenged both industry and the old-line craft unions of the American Federation of Labor. Massive sit-down strikes in the auto industry were, in large part, more successful than ever in terms of workers winning concessions. Longshoremen in San Francisco also led a huge general strike that spread from the waterfront to the whole city. The Maritime Union on the west coast subsequently grew in strength and militancy. These worker actions and movements grew out of a conviction that taking almost any action was better than accepting conditions as they were.[184]

It is also important to note that many American volunteers who went to Spain who were older than the age of 30 (more than a third of them) had often participated in radical movements in the decades between World War I and the Spanish War. Their conflicts with bossism during the Great Depression provided a crucial bridge – a living tradition – between a fading sense of the American Dream that had so long provided the ballast for notions of American identity.[185] The war in Spain was, in short, for many American volunteers, the next logical step from the class war being

---

[184] Hank Rubin, foreword by Peter N. Carroll, *Spain's Cause Was Mine: A Memoir of an American Medic in the Spanish Civil War* (Carbondale, Southern Illinois University Press, 1997) 8.

[185] Peter N. Carroll, *The Odyssey of the Abraham Lincoln Brigade: Americans in the Spanish Civil War* (Stanford, CA: Stanford University Press, 1994) 20.

waged between workers and employers in U.S. cities such as New York, Chicago and San Francisco.

Steve Nelson's *The Volunteers* (1953), for example, begins with a scene of abuse at the hands of Chicago's "Red Squad" before transitioning into Spain.[186] The language of class warfare was particularly prominent in Nelson's memoir and numerous letters written by American volunteers to loved ones. "Please write often," Dartmouth graduate and labor organizer Joe Dallet pleaded with his wife from a French prison where he and other volunteers were detained for trying to illegally enter Spain. "Remember what letters mean to class war prisoners," he reminded her.[187] Most of the volunteers, like Dallet, were men already heavily involved in labor unions, political movements, student-action groups, and/or Popular Front organizations. Spain merely reflected the depth of their dedication to social equality in the U.S. In Spain, the class conflicts of the preceding decade congealed into the idea of democracy for the proverbial people versus monarchial fascism as a kind of industrialized redux of the caste system associated with the Ancient Regime.

Long before leaving the U.S. for Spain, more than one third of the American volunteers had witnessed violence and physical abuse and in many

---

[186] Steve Nelson, *The Volunteers* (New York, Masses & Mainstream, 1953).

[187] Joe Dallet, April 2 1937, Perpignan Jail, "Letters From Spain, American Volunteer to His Wife" (New York, Workers Library Publishers, 1938). 15. Box 2, folder 60. Tamiment Library/Robert F. Wagner Labor Archives. Elmer Holmes Tamiment Library, 70 Washington Square South, New York NY 10012, New York University Libraries.

cases death of co-workers or unionists along picket-lines comprised of proletariats doing battle with both public and private police forces, hired strike breakers, thugs, spies and sundry other agent provocateurs who often used tear gas, machine guns, billie clubs, and firearms to defend the economic and political status quo in industrializing American cities during the Interwar Era. Violence was especially prominent from 1934 and after when unions were increasingly emboldened to pressure employers for greater transparency and fairness resulting from the first New Deal's National Industrial Recovery Act. Fascist forces in Spain were, many American volunteers believed, the same reactionary forces trying to crush unionization in the U.S. during the Great Depression.

After the rise of the IWW and other international labor unions, violent reprisals against American workers by employers were often considered one-in-the-same with the oppression of industrial workers in Germany, Italy, France, Latin America, Spain and many other cities throughout the world. As such, for many members of the International Brigades, going to Spain was an inevitable part of the union battles workers all over the world had seen firsthand in their home countries.[188]

In August, 1937 Bob Shissler, a former Columbia University undergrad, wrote a letter to friends in Johnstown, Pennsylvania, that connected the Spanish

---

[188] Robert A. Rosenstone, "The Men of the Abraham Lincoln Battalion," *The Journal of American History*, Vol. 54, No. 2 (Sep., 1967), pp. 327-338.

War with battles between workers and employers in the U.S.:

> When you read of the victories on the battlefields of Spain – try to realize in part the fact that every victory there means an even greater victory in the rear by all the people. And if you want the answer to the future – it is being written gloriously by all the people now. For today's victory in the rear is tomorrow's victory in the field… We consider your success there necessary for our success here. And we depend on you. All of us look forward to the day when our task is completed here and we can come back and put our shoulders to the wheel…
> Carry on your fight comrades – as we will here. In our hands will rest the destruction of fascism and the triumph of the workers of the whole world.[189]

Some letters, such as Shissler's, specifically alluded to volunteers' identification with labor and

---

[189] Bob Shissler, August 26, 1937, Soccoro Rojo, Albacete, Spain. His letter also stated. "It would be impossible for me to picture the joy and satisfaction that comes to all the boys with the issue of American cigarettes and chocolate and all the other things you can send through the "friends," nor can we forget the point that such an organization is of unlimited assistance in utilizing our presence here – in rallying support to the cause of Republican Spain – in raising international solidarity behind democracy as a practical problem of the working class." Tamiment Library/Robert F. Wagner Labor Archives. Elmer Holmes Tamiment Library, 70 Washington Square South, New York NY 10012, New York University Libraries. Shissler was born November 19, 1909. He sailed June 2, 1937 aboard the *Aquitania*. He was killed in action October 13, 1937 at Fuentes de Ebro.

political organizations throughout the world. "We had come (to Spain) because of a deep feeling that to take up the fight here was the logical step from our battles on the picket lines," Earl Luppo wrote from the Jarama Front in May, 1937.[190] "We are overjoyed with the progress of the CIO in the major industries," Andrew Pape wrote from a trench somewhere outside Madrid in July 1937; "America is marching forward and we are marching with America on the battlefields of Spain," he added. "There is more than one front for democracy in the world today and America is in the forefront on many of them."[191]

Morris Stamm, a labor organizer from Cleveland, similarly expressed that the war in Spain "was a struggle in the same sense as workers struggle in order to be able to choose the way of life they desire against the owners who impose on them the kind of oppression and totalitarian control of their working hours and therefore of their life in general," he wrote. "This is why there is a real similarity between fascism and bossism. And that is why I went to fight in Spain, as part of a class struggle."[192] University of Washington

---

[190] Earl Luppo, Jarama Front, May 8, 1937, in "From the Cradle of Liberty to the Tomb of Fascism: Letters from Philadelphians Fighting in Spain," M.H. Wickman, Al Handler, Leo Kaufman, Harold London, Ed Ahern, J. Drill, Karl Samuels (Philadelphia, The Communist Party of Eastern Pennsylvania, 1937) 8.

[191] Andrew Pape, July 10, 1937, published in "From the Cradle of Liberty to the Tomb of Fascism: Letters from Philadelphians Fighting in Spain," (Philadelphia, The Communist Party of Eastern Pennsylvania, 1937) 21.

[192] Morris Stamm oral history as quoted in John Gerassi, *The Premature Antifascists: North American Volunteers in*

grad, John Lucid, likewise wrote friends back home that, "To make Spain the tomb of fascism demands all our energy, all our devotion, special responsibility on the vanguard of the working class."[193]

Although there were some volunteers who went for adventure or out of a desperation to escape the Great Depression, and some who went on impulse, the vast majority of American volunteers "left their own country (which they loved) as a result of the irresistible determination to take their place in a struggle whose frontlines are not confined to Spain," Alvah Bessie wrote in his 1939 memoir. Wilfred Mendelson likewise wrote to his folks a year earlier, in June 1938, that "our bunch, a true cross-section of America, auto workers from Detroit, steel men from McKeesport and Pittsburgh, sailors and longshoremen, are quite united and this will certainly show good results at the front."[194] For many American volunteers, as the excerpts from letters above especially indicate, the war in Spain was an extension of the labor struggles waged on U.S. soil during the Progressive era and especially during the decades after

---

the Spanish Civil War 1936-39: An Oral History (New York, Praeger, 1986) 78-79.

[193] John Lucid letter to Queens Committee, Young Communist League, New York, N.Y., February 24, 1938, John Lucid papers: ALBA.206. Tamiment Library/Robert F. Wagner Labor Archives. Elmer Holmes Tamiment Library, 70 Washington Square South, New York NY 10012, New York University Libraries.

[194] Wilfred Mendelson, June 22, 1938, in Cary Nelson and Jefferson Hicks, eds. *Madrid 1937: Letters of the Abraham Lincoln Brigade From the Spanish Civil War* (New York, Routledge, 1996) 40.

World War I, which helps explain why the U.S. government was officially neutral all throughout the war in Spain, despite the fact that the overwhelming majority of Americans polled wished the fascists would ultimately lose the war.

Integral to the class war waged in American cities and its extension into war with fascists in Spain was the race hatred that helped justify workplace and residential apartheid throughout the world. Part and parcel of the global class struggle central to the Spanish War was the racism fascists obsessively represented and propagated as a means of arbitrarily dividing and conquering the world's working classes. Many American volunteers went to Spain as a reaction to the world around them – the Great Depression, the organization of labor unions, and the potential threat to freedom posed by European Fascism, which was fundamentally anti-labor, anti-Semitic, anti-intellectual, and in stark contrast to Enlightenment Era ideals such as liberty, equality and fraternity.

Of the volunteers to Spain from the U.S., about a third to forty percent were Jewish, with the proportion among medical personnel as high as sixty-two percent of the surgeons/physicians, seventy-five percent of the oral surgeons, and fifty-eight percent of nurses.[195] Although many Lincolns were Jewish, few were orthodox. They

---

[195] Hank Rubin, foreword by Peter N. Carroll, *Spain's Cause Was Mine: A Memoir of an American Medic in the Spanish Civil War* (Carbondale, Southern Illinois University Press, 1997) 14. See also Alan Stuart Rockman, "Jewish Participation in the International Brigades in the Spanish Civil War, 1936-1939." MA Thesis, California State University, Fullerton, 1981.

were often agnostics or atheists – who in the 1930s were attracted to Popular Front organizations not only because they were opposing Hitler, but also because the CPUSA promised to break the old forms of society that traditionally meant oppression for American Jews. The International Brigades, particularly the American volunteers, seemed to offer Jewish volunteers a community in which all men were equal and in which they could shed the limitations of their social reality and "join in a fraternity that transcended the divisions of the world."[196]

Many Jewish-American volunteers were educated and therefore likely cognizant of the inquisition that had forced Semites out of the Iberian Peninsula centuries earlier and were thus particularly invested in stopping fascism in Spain. Hyman Katz, a volunteer from New York City, went to Spain without telling his mother because he did not want to upset her. But when he was wounded in action in 1937, the young volunteer's service in Spain was reported in the popular press and he was reluctantly compelled to explain to her why he had defied her wishes by enlisting with the International Brigades:

---

[196] Jewish members of the Battalion can be identified simply on the basis of names. Of the 1,804 men identified, 371 (20.6 percent) had obviously Jewish names. Since many changed their names to go to Spain and since all Jews do not have "Jewish" names, the 25 percent estimate seems warranted. This estimate was confirmed by various interviewees, Jews and non-Jews alike, such as Bill Bailey, Benjamin Sills, and John Lucid. Also Steve Nelson interview at New York, Aug. 1, 1964. See also Robert A. Rosenstone, "The Men of the Abraham Lincoln Battalion," *The Journal of American History*, Vol. 54, No. 2 (Sep., 1967), pp. 327-338, p. 334.

I came to Spain because I felt I had to. Look at the world situation. We didn't worry when Mussolini came to power in Italy. We felt bad when Hitler became Chancellor of Germany, but what could we do? We felt –though we tried to help and sympathize – that it was their problem and wouldn't affect us. Then the fascist governments sent out agents and began to gain power in other countries. Remember the anti-Semitic troubles in Austria only about a year ago. Look at what is happening in Poland; and see how the fascists are increasing their power in the Balkans – and Greece -- and how the Italians are trying to play up to the Arab leaders... Seeing all these things – how fascism is grasping power in many countries (including the U.S., where there are many Nazi organizations and Nazi agents and spies) – can't you see that fascism is our problem – that it may come to us as it came in other countries? And don't you realize that we Jews will be the first to suffer if fascism comes? But if we didn't see clearly the hand of Mussolini and Hitler in all these countries, in Spain we can't help seeing it. Together with their agent, Franco, they are trying to set up the same anti-progressive, anti-Semitic regime in Spain, as they have in Italy and Germany... If we sit by and let them grow stronger by taking Spain, they will move on to France and will not stop there; and it won't be long before they get to America. Realizing this, can I sit by and wait until the beasts get to my very door – until it is too late, and there is no one I can call on for help? And would I even deserve help from others when the trouble comes upon me, if I were to refuse help to those who need it today? If I permitted such a time to come – as a Jew and a progressive, I would be among the first to fall under the axe of the fascists; all I could do then would be to curse myself and say, "Why didn't I wake up when the alarm-clock rang?" But then it would be too late – just as it was too late for the Jews in Germany to find out in 1933 that they were wrong in believing that Hitler would never rule Germany... So I took up arms against the persecutors of my people – the Jews – and my class – the Oppressed. I am fighting against those who establish an inquisition like that of their ideological ancestors several centuries ago, in Spain. Are these traits which you admire so much in a Prophet Jeremiah or a Judas Maccabeus, bad when your son exhibits them? I'm trying with my own meager capabilities, to do what they did with their great capabilities, in the struggle for Liberty, well-being, and Peace.[197]

A June 1938 letter by New Yorker Wilfred Mendelson to his parents also underscored the centrality of Jewish

---

[197] Hyman Katz, November 11, 1937, "Letter from the Front in Spain," *Jewish Currents,* XL (February 1979), pp. 4-6, 16-17. Tamiment Library/Robert F. Wagner Labor Archives. Elmer Holmes Tamiment Library, 70 Washington Square South, New York NY 10012, New York University Libraries. Katz sailed on the *Queen Mary.* He arrived in Spain July 24, 1937. He was killed in action in Belchite, March 3, 1938 during the Retreats.

identity in compelling him and many others to volunteer to fight fascism in Spain:

> The real international language here (among the International Brigades) is Yiddish. Jews from Germany, France, England, Poland, Czech, Hungary, Romania, all the front ranks of their respective movements have come to battle the common enemy of the workers, and of the Jews as a special oppressed minority... Spain is perhaps a fit arena for this struggle. Here it was that the Medieval Inquisition drove the Jews from their homes and their livelihoods. Today Jews are returning welcomed by the entire Spanish people to fight the modern Inquisition, and in many cases the direct descendants of the ancient persecution – the Catholic Jesuit hierarchy – the feudal landholders combined with the finance capitalist oligarchy... I am sure we are fighting in the best Maccabean tradition.[198]

---

[198] Wilfred Mendelson, June 22, 1938, in Cary Nelson and Jefferson Hicks, eds. *Madrid 1937: Letters of the Abraham Lincoln Brigade From the Spanish Civil War* (New York, Routledge, 1996) 40. The "maccabean tradition" invoked by Mendelson and Katz dates back to 168 BCE, when the ruler of the Syrian kingdom, Antiochus Epiphanes IV, stepped up his campaign to quash Judaism, so that all subjects in his vast empire–which included the Land of Israel–would share the same culture and worship the same gods. He marched into Jerusalem, vandalized the Temple, erected an idol on the altar, and desecrated its holiness with the blood of swine. Decreeing that studying Torah, observing the Sabbath, and circumcising Jewish boys were punishable by death, he sent Syrian overseers and soldiers to villages throughout Judea to enforce the edicts and force Jews to engage in idol worship. When the Syrian soldiers reached Modin (about 12 miles northwest of

Hank Rubin's Jewish heritage was also especially central to his eagerness to fight fascism in Spain. "I was angered that so many Jews had let themselves be annihilated or degraded in Czarist Russia without fighting back," he wrote in his memoir. "My father and his family had not fought back but had left Ukraine and moved to the U.S.... As a Jew and an American, I felt responsibility to fight against anti-Semitism and fascism."[199] Rubin also, as many black and white American volunteers were apt to do, made the connection between oppression of Jews around the world with the oppression of African

---

the capital), they demanded that the local leader, Mattathias the *Kohein* (a member of the priestly class), be an example to his people by sacrificing a pig on a portable pagan altar. The elder refused and killed not only the Jew who stepped forward to do the Syrian's bidding, but also the king's representative. With the rallying cry "Whoever is for God, follow me!" Mattathias and his five sons (Jonathan, Simon, Judah, Eleazar, and Yohanan) fled to the hills and caves of the wooded Judean wilderness. Joined by a ragtag army of others like them, simple farmers dedicated to the laws of Moses, armed only with spears, bows and arrows, and rocks from the terrain, the Maccabees, as Mattathias' sons, particularly Judah, came to be known, fought a guerilla war against the well-trained, well-equipped, seemingly endless forces of the mercenary Syrian army. In three years, the Maccabees cleared the way back to the Temple mount, which they reclaimed. They cleaned the Temple and dismantled the defiled altar and constructed a new one in its place. Three years to the day after Antiochus' mad rampage *(Kislev* 25, 165 BCE), the Maccabees held a dedication*(hanukkah)* of the Temple with proper sacrifice, rekindling of the golden *menorah,* and eight days of celebration and praise to God. [Proper] Jewish worship had been reestablished.

[199] Hank Rubin, foreword by Peter N. Carroll, *Spain's Cause Was Mine: A Memoir of an American Medic in the Spanish Civil War* (Carbondale, Southern Illinois University Press, 1997) 14 and 16.

Americans in the U.S. "I had nothing but disdain for the hypocrisy of decrying anti-Semitism and then in the next breath railing in a racist way against blacks," Rubin wrote.[200]

By the mid-1930s many American volunteers, especially black and Jewish workers, had grown increasingly cognizant of the connection that the lynching of African Americans in the South was evidence of fascism and terrorism within the U.S. and that racism was ultimately an imminent threat to working-class solidarity throughout the nation and world. "What was it that sent us two-thousand-and-seven-hundred Americans to Spain? Could it have been the six pesetas per day (30 cents) that we often returned to the Spanish Government so that the fight against fascism might be continued?" Herbert Burton wrote. "No. It was not so. It was really because we now realized that fascism must come to an end in order that the peoples of the world would be free," he added. "Not only Jews, but the Negro and other oppressed nationalities."[201]

In 1937 Canute Frankson, an African-American volunteer, likewise explained that:

---

[200] Hank Rubin, foreword by Peter N. Carroll, *Spain's Cause Was Mine: A Memoir of an American Medic in the Spanish Civil War* (Carbondale, Southern Illinois University Press, 1997) 15.

[201] Herbert Burton in Steve Nelson Box 4, Folder: Herbert Burton, Jews in the International Brigade (1937). Tamiment Library/Robert F. Wagner Labor Archives. Elmer Holmes Tamiment Library, 70 Washington Square South, New York NY 10012, New York University Libraries.

> If fascism gains power in America we and the Jews will be the baits... The final victory is dependent on the international aid we get. The harder the blow here against the fascist beast, the easier it'll be to extract his teeth at home...We must not fall into the trap of racial isolationism That's just what the enemy wants us to do. We are part of the American progressive movement. We have one common enemy, and can only win by uniting our forces. Anyone who opposes unity, consciously or unconsciously, is our enemy. Whether he is black or white does not matter. The Negro who opposes unity while he preaches race loyalty and race consciousness is by far the worst of the enemies.[202]

American Volunteers, both black and white, also increasingly connected Hitler's fascism with the racism that had for so long helped define American culture during the antebellum period through the Jim Crow era in U.S. history.

Harlem resident Vaughn Love, one of nearly a hundred African Americans who volunteered to fight fascism in Spain, explained the connection between race hatred of Jews and blacks as a reason for volunteering to fight in Spain. "I'd read Hitler's book," he wrote, "knew about the Nuremburg laws, and I knew if the Jews weren't going to be allowed to live, then certainly I

---

[202] Canute Frankson to friend, July 23, 1937, Steve Nelson Box 1, Folder, Canute Frankson Letters From Spain. Tamiment Library/Robert F. Wagner Labor Archives. Elmer Holmes Tamiment Library, 70 Washington Square South, New York NY 10012, New York University Libraries.

knew the Negroes would not escape."[203] Before he was killed at Brunete in 1937, he was promoted to commander of the Lincoln-Washington Battalion, becoming the first black officer ever to command a predominately white battalion of American soldiers in battle.

A decade before the end of de jure Jim Crow in the U.S. Armed Forces, black volunteers fought side-by-side and shared trenches and foxholes with white compatriots in the first fully integrated (albeit unofficial) American fighting force.[204] African-American volunteers were full and equal partners with their white compatriots, with the democratic Spaniards, and with like-minded allies from around the globe. And despite the horror and deprivation intrinsic to war, African-American volunteer Tom Page fondly remembered "the feeling of human dignity… and the feeling of camaraderie. This was Spain's meaning to me… It's the first time in my life I was treated with human dignity… treated as a human being, as man."[205]

In August of 1941, fewer than four months before Japan bombed Pearl Harbor, Albert Prago, a

---

[203] Peter N. Carroll, *The Odyssey of the Abraham Lincoln Brigade: Americans in the Spanish Civil War* (Stanford, CA: Stanford University Press, 1994), and Fraser Ottanelli in Peter N. Carroll & James D. Fernadez, *Facing Fascism: New York & The Spanish Civil War* (New York, NYU Press, 2007), 79.

[204] Danny Duncan Collum, editor, and Victor A. Berch, Chief Researcher, *African Americans in the Spanish Civil War: "This Ain't Ethiopia, But It Will Do"* (New York, G.K. Hall and Company, 1992) 5.

[205] Tom Page in Alvah Bessie and Albert Prago, eds. *Our Fight: Writing of the Abraham Lincoln Brigade Spain 1936 - 1939* (New York, Monthly Review Press, 1987) 55.

Jewish-American volunteer, justified his involvement fighting fascism in Spain by using the solidarity between black and white volunteers as a kind of moral highground in contrast to the pervasive institutionalized racism in the U.S., which he felt was synonymous with global fascism. He wrote:

> To ensure a genuine fight against Hitlerism, we demand an ousting of those officers who are fascist-minded; we demand the democratization of the Army. Wipe out the disgraceful stigma of Jim Crow in the Army! What a travesty on the concept of democracy to segregate one antifascist soldier from another because of the color of his skin! Open up the ranks of the officers to all who qualify through merit and merit alone! Admit to the officer training schools all who qualify regardless of race, creed, color or social origin![206]

---

[206] Albert Prago, *We Fought Hitler* (New York, Veterans of the Abraham Lincoln Brigade, August 1941) 11. Prago was born in New York City in 1911. His parents were Latvian Jewish immigrants to the United States. Although his upbringing was not religious, he explained in an interview that his desire to volunteer to fight fascism had its roots in his Jewish cultural identity, an identity that is reflected in his later research on Jewish involvement in the Spanish Civil War. He joined the Communist Party in 1934. Before his departure for Spain in 1937, he was a charter member of Local 453, American Federation of Teachers, and taught social sciences in the Works Projects Administration adult education project. While a member of the Lincoln Brigade, he served both as Anglo-American editor of the International Brigades' daily newsletter and as the battalion's interpreter. Prago was wounded in the thigh by mortar fire during the second battle of Belchite in March 1938, and complications from osteomyelitis required him to spend over a year in the hospital before his recovery was complete. After his return to New York in 1938, Prago

Prago's foresighted demand helps demonstrate how idealistic many American volunteers were, but also how far ahead of the proverbial curve they were in regard to the evolution of the federal government after World War II. The American volunteers were the first to fight fascism – in defiance of their own government, no less. They were also at the forefront of demanding an end to racial segregation within the Armed Forces, which was revolutionary idealism.[207]

During the Great Depression, black and white American volunteers such as Prago, Page and many others, together with liberal-minded intellectuals, scholars, and artists, such as George Orwell and Langston Hughes, were increasingly connecting oppression of the world's workers with race-hatred. "All of them are here because they know that as fascism creeps across Spain, across Europe, and then across the world, there will be no place left for intelligent young

---

concentrated his efforts on teaching and research, and remained deeply involved in radical political activity. He eventually earned a Ph.D. in history at the age of 65 from Union Institute and University, and taught at the Jefferson School of Social Science, Hofstra University, Cornell University's N.Y.State School of Industrial and Labor Relations, Empire State College, and the New School for Social Research. His publications on the Spanish Civil War and the International Brigades include several articles exploring the roles of Jews and women in the conflict; these are collected in the 1987 anthology Our Fight: Writings by Veterans of the Abraham Lincoln Brigade, Spain 1936-1939 co-edited by Prago and Alvah Bessie. Prago retired to West Palm Beach, Florida. He continued to publish historical articles and remained actively involved with the Veterans of the Abraham Lincoln Brigade until his death from cancer in July 1993.

[207] The U.S. Armed Forces was finally integrated in 1948.

Negroes at all," Hughes wrote in a 1937 editorial published in the Lincoln Battalion newsletter, *Volunteer For Liberty*. "In fact, no decent place for any Negroes – because fascism preaches the creed of Nordic supremacy and a world for whites alone."[208]

Almost all of the black volunteers and many whites had confronted racism, poverty and oppression long before going to Spain. While the Depression was a time of widespread suffering and social injustice for millions of white Americans, its impact on the vast majority of black Americans was even more profound. The circumstances of economic collapse and deprivation led many African Americans to seek equality in the founding of a new economic order that would put peoples' needs before the demands of profit. This economic struggle brought black Americans into alliance with counterparts from other races, and ultimately led to the formation of bi-racial labor organizations, unemployed councils, and tenant unions, which increased workers' ability to successfully collectively bargain with management.

Langston Hughes, who traveled to Spain in 1937 as a correspondent for the *Baltimore Afro-American* and as a contributor for the *Volunteer For Liberty*, likewise alluded to fascism as a kind of redux of slavery. His speech, "Too Much Race," delivered at the Second

---

[208] Langston Hughes, "Negroes in Spain" *Volunteer For Liberty* 1, no.14 (September 13, 1937) in Danny Duncan Collum, editor, and Victor A. Berch, Chief Researcher, *African Americans in the Spanish Civil War: "This Ain't Ethiopia, But It Will Do"* (New York, G.K. Hall and Company, 1992) 103.

International Writers Congress in Paris in July 1937, explained:

> I come from a land called America, a democratic land, a rich land – and yet a land whose democracy from the very beginning has been tainted with race prejudice born of slavery, and whose richness has been poured through the narrow channels of greed into the hands of the few. I come to the second International Writers Congress to represent my country, America, but most especially representing the Negro peoples of America, and the poor peoples of America – because I am both a Negro and poor. And that combination of color and poverty gives me the right to speak for the most oppressed group in America – that group that has known so little of democracy – the fifteen million Negroes who dwell within our borders… We are the people who have long known in actual practice the meaning of the word fascism – for the attitude toward us has always been one of economic and social discrimination… We know Jim Crow cars, race riots, lynchings, the sorrows of the Scottsboro boys… We Negroes of America are tired of a world divided superficially in the basis of race and color – but in reality, on the basis of poverty and power – the rich over the poor, no matter what their color.[209]

---

[209] Langston Hughes, "Too Much Race," July 1937, Second International Writers Congress, Paris, in Danny Duncan Collum, editor, and Victor A. Berch, Chief Researcher, *African Americans in the Spanish Civil War: "This Ain't Ethiopia, But It Will Do"* (New York, G.K. Hall and Company, 1992) 106. The Scottsboro Boys were nine African-American teenagers

Hughes' sentiment was seconded in a letter written by Frankson in July, 1937, the same month as the International Writers Congress:

> All we have to do is think of the lynching of our people. We can look back at the pages of American history stained with the blood of Negroes; stink with the burning bodies of our people hanging from tress; bitter with the groans of our tortured loved ones from whose living bodies, ears, fingers, toes have been cut for souvenirs – living bodies into which red-hot pokers have been thrust.... if we crush fascism here, we'll save our people in America, and in other parts of the world, from the vicious persecution, wholesale imprisonment, and slaughter which the Jewish people suffered and are suffering under Hitler's fascist heels.[210]

In other words, although the economy had changed in many regards from the days when agrarianism was the primary locust of economic accumulation and wealth creation, power relations had not much changed as a

---

accused in Alabama of raping two White American women on a train in 1931. The landmark set of legal cases from this incident dealt with racism and the right to a fair trial. The cases included a lynch mob before the suspects had been indicted, a frame-up, all-white juries, rushed trials, and disruptive mobs. It is frequently cited as an example of an overall miscarriage of justice in the United States legal system.

[210] Canute Frankson to friend, July 6, 1937, Albacete, Spain, in Steve Nelson Box 1, Folder, Canute Frankson Letters From Spain June 26, 1937. Tamiment Library/Robert F. Wagner Labor Archives. Elmer Holmes Tamiment Library, 70 Washington Square South, New York NY 10012, New York University Libraries.

result of industrialization and urbanization. In fact, many perceived fascism to be an industrialization of the feudalistic power relations of the antebellum era. Jim Crow was all the evidence many needed. Take for example an excerpt from a letter written by M.H. Wickman in May, 1937:

> Tell the Negro people that their side of freedom is with the Spanish anti-fascists – with the oppressed of all lands united in Spain to make a tomb of fascism here. Appeals should be made to the Negro organizations for immediate action, for unity, for greater sacrifice. We find among the best fighters here the Negro anti-fascists. Many are leading and holding high positions who yesterday were strangers and today are the living symbol of united actions.[211]

The war in Spain, in short, provided one more opportunity for African Americans to expose the farcical "logic" of blacks' supposed inferiority that provided fascists in the Jim Crow South and in northern cities their rationale. For millions of people across the globe, especially oppressed people of color and working-class whites, Spain was emblematic of a global struggle against the same pervasive exploitation, racism, and

---

[211] M.H. Wickman, May 17, 1937, "From the Cradle of Liberty to the Tomb of Fascism: Letters from Philadelphians Fighting in Spain," M.H. Wickman, Al Handler, Leo Kaufman, Harold London, Ed Ahern, J. Drill, Karl Samuels (Philadelphia, The Communist Party of Eastern Pennsylvania, 1937) 11. Wickman was a seamen and longshoreman. He joined the CP in 1930, and was a prominent leader in Philadelphia. He left for Spain aboard the *Washington,* March 10, 1937. He was wounded July 19, 1937 by nationalist aircraft during the Brunete offensive and died as a result.

class inequity that was based on arbitrary social divisions that had existed since long before the French, American and Russian Revolutions.

Many African Americans who volunteered to fight fascism in Spain, such as Frankson, Love, Page, and Vaughn, especially saw their participation in the anti-fascist struggle as part of a larger campaign to extend black Americans' claims to equality and self-determination in the U.S. and throughout the world. In other words, the National Association for the Advancement of Colored People's Double-V campaign, which was so prominent during World War II, was being forged by black and white American volunteers in Spain. In July 1937, for example, Frankson wrote:

> We are no longer an isolated minority group fighting hopelessly against an immense giant. On the battlefields of Spain, we fight for the preservation of democracy. Here we're laying the foundation for world peace, and for the liberation of my people, and of the human race. We have joined with, and become an active part of, a great progressive force, on whose shoulders rests the responsibility of saving human civilization from the planned destruction of a small group of degenerates gone mad in their lust for power.[212]

---

[212] Canute Frankson to friend, July 6, 1937, Albacete, Spain, in Steve Nelson Box 1, Folder, Canute Frankson Letters From Spain June 26, 1937. Tamiment Library/Robert F. Wagner Labor Archives. Elmer Holmes Tamiment Library, 70 Washington Square South, New York NY 10012, New York University Libraries.

The first-hand experience of racist persecution by African Americans in the U.S. led many to identify strongly with poverty stricken white victims of European Fascism. The Black Left in general, which was increasingly Pan-African, and African-American volunteers in particular, saw nationalism and internationalism as two sides of the same ideological coin. African-American volunteers such as Frankson and Love were often as heavily influenced by the Depression Era Popular Front as they were by Black Nationalism, and African-American folk culture. Many African Americans who went to Spain were at their core motivated by a long-range concern for the welfare of their own communities, which was increasingly global in scope. Again and again, that message is evoked in correspondence written by black volunteers, in which they connect the invasion of Ethiopia by Mussolini as a key factor in determining their decision to go Spain. Many African-American volunteers knew that in Spain they would have the opportunity to do battle with the same Italian Army that had massacred Ethiopians just two years earlier.[213]

By the mid-point of the Spanish War, working-class African Americans, Jewish Americans, white scholars, artists and intellectuals all across the globe, including luminaries as bright as George Orwell and Langston Hughes, were increasingly finding solidarity rooted in centuries of social and economic inequity

---

[213] For more on Mussolini and Italy's invasion of Spain see Danny Duncan Collum, editor, and Victor A. Berch, Chief Researcher, *African Americans in the Spanish Civil War: "This Ain't Ethiopia, But It Will Do"* (New York, G.K. Hall and Company, 1992) 190.

rationalized and perpetuated in part by racism. "In country after country, the organized working-class movements have been crushed by open, illegal violence," Orwell wrote in 1943. "The forced-labour [sic] camps all over Europe and North Africa where Poles, Russians, Jews and political prisoners of every race toil at road-making or swamp-draining for their bare rations, are simple chattel slavery."[214]

In other words, black and white volunteers found continuity in economic and political exploitation from antebellum agrarianism through to 1930s industrialization.[215] In his 1939 memoir, *Men in Battle*, Alvah Bessie, for instance, wrote, "We are faced within the borders of our own country, with a 'dynamic crusade' to destroy the liberties of the American people in the name of 'national security.' We are faced with a desperate attempt to return the American worker to the

---

[214] George Orwell "Looking back on the Spanish War." He also evoked the trend towards social history by writing, "those hundreds of millions of slaves on whose backs civilization rested generation after generation have left behind them no record whatever. We do not even know their names."

[215] In 1859 Brown led a raid on the federal armory at Harpers Ferry. During the raid, he seized the armory; seven people were killed, and ten or more were injured. He intended to arm slaves with weapons from the arsenal, but the attack failed. Within 36 hours, Brown's men had fled or been killed or captured by local pro-slavery farmers, militiamen, and U.S. Marines led by Robert E. Lee. Brown's subsequent capture by federal forces seized the nation's attention, as Southerners feared it was just the first of many Northern plots to cause a slave rebellion that might endanger their lives, while Republicans dismissed the notion and said they would not interfere with slavery in the South.

days of the open shop; to deny the American Negro people their rightful place in society."[216]

Spain was thus not simply another "white man's war;" it was, for many volunteers, an extension of the Italo-Ethiopian conflict, as well as the American and French Revolutions. But it was also integrally related to the power and economic relations between owners and workers rooted in antebellum era slavery. As Hughes' poem "October 16th," which commemorated John Brown's raid on the U.S. Army arsenal at Harper's Ferry in 1859 and the Lincolns naming of an artillery company after John Brown helps illuminate, black and white volunteers identified their fight as a continuation of the antebellum emancipationists' cause, which was rooted in Enlightenment Era ideas and discourse – particularly freedom and self-determination for all, regardless of class or race.

---

[216] Alvah Bessie, *Men in Battle: A Story of Americans in Spain*, (New York, Scribner, 1939) xviii.

Chapter Seven

"Volunteers for Fraternity"

The Greek philosopher Aristotle, whose ideas influenced the Enlightenment, divided friendship into three types, based on the motive for forming them: friendships of utility, friendships of pleasure, and friendships of the good. Friendships of utility and friendships of the good, which are defined by philia – brotherly love – are pronounced in many of the American volunteers' correspondence to friends and family during the Spanish War. Their friends and family likewise tended to believe the American volunteers were genuinely invested in making the world a better and safer place for all humanity. Stewart French, roommate of volunteer, Thomas Donato Petrella, at Harvard and in New York City in the early 1930s, wrote to John Hutchinson who had inquired about Petrella's whereabouts after his disappearance in Spain. In a letter dated December 9, 1938, French wrote:

> To the best of my knowledge, Tom died of battle wounds received while fighting for democracy against fascism in Spain, as a member of the Abraham Lincoln battalion. I heard from him from Spain regularly until about a year ago when I saw a notice in the *New York Times* that he had been wounded, and all letters stopped. Subsequent efforts to locate him have failed… I feel earnestly that every member of the Harvard class of 1929, regardless of his beliefs or religious affiliations, should feel proud of Tom

Petrella who died gallantly for his faith – that of the brotherhood of man.[217]

Many soldiers in many wars have often expressed a genuine brotherhood with those they go into battle with. Despite the numerous nationalities, and various levels of education and socioeconomic privileges of the International Brigades, including the American volunteers, many letters expressed a genuine love for other men in the trenches. "I wanted to work (for the first time) in a large body of men," Alvah Bessie wrote in the notebook that became the basis of his 1939 memoir, *Men in Battle*, "to submerge myself in the mass, seeking neither distinction nor preferment – the obverse of my activities the past several years – and in this way to achieve: self-discipline, patience, resignation and unselfishness."[218]

But this longing for selflessness extended far beyond merely wanting to be part of a body of men at war. What is especially striking about many of the American volunteers' letters is the prevalent expression of philia for the people of the world, Spanish Republicans, and especially other Americans – as well as their comrades in arms. American volunteers' letters, as

---

[217] Stewart French to John Hutchinson. December 9, 1938, New York City. Thomas D. Petrella, from Buffalo, NY, was A.B. Cum laude, Harvard, class of 1929. Petrella sailed March 10, 1937 aboard the *Queen Mary*. He was killed in action September 6, 1937. Petrella Papers: ALBA.252. Tamiment Library/Robert F. Wagner Labor Archives. Elmer Holmes Tamiment Library, 70 Washington Square South, New York NY 10012, New York University Libraries.

[218] Alvah Bessie, edited by Dan Bessie, *Alvah Bessie's Spanish Civil War Notebooks* (Lexington, University of Kentucky Press).

earlier pages have elaborated, often expressed the belief that they were fighting for liberty and equality in Spain. But many letters also expressed a genuine belief in fraternity for the people of the world, particularly workers, the Spanish people, and especially for fellow Americans, which was defined by a profound concern for the future of the United States as a whole during the Great Depression, which was manifested in trepidation of being pulled into another cataclysmic World War. Fighting in Spain, many American volunteers believed, was necessary in preventing World War II, which to many seemed inevitable without the intervention of the other western democracies.

"The most important thing in the world is to advance the cause of the working people at home, to unite it and lead it so that fascism will never have a chance in America," American volunteer John Field, who was a track and cross-country star at the University of Rochester before graduating in 1935, wrote his mother in 1937.[219] Jack Friedman likewise wrote a friend in February 1937 expressing the conviction that, "aiding the Spanish people is one of the best ways to do it (preventing the spread of facism). We are pushed on by a certain knowledge that we are enlisted in a struggle

---

[219] John Field to his mother, October 9, 1937, SRI, Plaza del Altozano, Albacete, Spain. Box 2, folder 145, ALBA Vertical Files; Tamiment Library/Robert F. Wagner Labor Archives. Elmer Holmes Tamiment Library, 70 Washington Square South, New York NY 10012, New York University Libraries. Field was born in 1913 in Paraguay. His father, who also volunteered for the Spanish Republic, were members of the CP. He sailed for Spain aboard the *Queen Mary* and arrived in Spain June 18, 1937. He was killed in action January 18, 1938 in Teruel. He was a renowned track star in college at the University of Rochester.

that is for all humanity and one that must someday triumph."[220] Carl Geiser also wrote of the importance of his service to all humanity in a letter to his wife: "It is certainly interesting to meet people from every country in the world, all here to help the legal government of Spain drive out the fascist invaders, thus weaken world fascism and prevent a new world war – all recognize that the battle they are fighting now helps to keep the rest of the world, including their own country-men, out of war."[221] Joe Dallet similarly wrote his mother from Paris en route to Spain that:

> You know that I have been very much concerned with the situation in Spain. I profoundly believe that the military invasion of Hitler and Mussolini into Democratic Spain must receive a military defeat of the first order if the peace of Europe and the World is to be preserved and fascism is to be checked, instead of spread. If Hitler and Mussolini win in Spain, they attack next France (helped from within by the French fascists), Czechoslovakia, the USSR, etc. On the other hand, if the Spanish government wins, it is a severe defeat for fascism all over the world, and will immensely

---

[220] Jack Friedman, Saturday, Feb. 1937, in Cary Nelson and Jefferson Hicks, eds. *Madrid 1937: Letters of the Abraham Lincoln Brigade From the Spanish Civil War* (New York, Routledge, 1996) 43.

[221] Carl Geiser to Impy, May 20, 1937, Albacete, Spain; Carl Geiser Papers, ALBA.004, Folder: Outgoing Correspondence, April – May 1937. Tamiment Library/Robert F. Wagner Labor Archives. Elmer Holmes Tamiment Library, 70 Washington Square South, New York NY 10012, New York University Libraries.

assist the Italian and German people to overthrow the bloody yoke of terroristic dictatorship.[222]

A month later, after arriving in Spain, he wrote his mother again explaining:

> There is a wonderful gang of men here – the Int'l Brigade is assembled of men from 55 countries of the world – all united by a common purpose – to save Spain for democracy by defeating the military intervention of Hitler and Mussolini. There is such a bond of fellowship established that breaks down all national boundaries. French & German march and fight side by side.[223]

Irving Busch of Columbia College of Physicians likewise told a reporter: "We were a brotherhood united in a struggle for social justice."[224] A Bostonian named

---

[222] Joe Dallet to Mother, from Paris, March 19, 1937. Joe Dallet Papers, ALBA.032, Box 1, folder: 1937, Tamiment Library/Robert F. Wagner Labor Archives. Elmer Holmes Tamiment Library, 70 Washington Square South, New York NY 10012, New York University Libraries.

[223] Joe Dallet to Mother, from Albacete, Spain, April 25, 1937, Joe Dallet Papers, ALBA.032, Box 1, folder: 1937; Tamiment Library/Robert F. Wagner Labor Archives. Elmer Holmes Tamiment Library, 70 Washington Square South, New York NY 10012, New York University Libraries.

[224] Irving Busch quoted in news clipping from *Valley News*, 13, April, 1981 in Joe Dallet's folder, vertical files, box 3, folder 60. Tamiment Library/Robert F. Wagner Labor Archives. Elmer Holmes Tamiment Library, 70 Washington Square South, New York NY 10012, New York University Libraries. Busch was born August 24, 1896 in New York City. He graduated from Columbia University College of Physicians

Charley O'Flaherty, who went to Spain with two of his brothers, rejoiced in a letter home that, "We had quite a few I.R.A. (the Irish Republic Army, which waged a long and bitterly fought war with the British empire) men with us. They're the best soldiers."[225] M.H. Wickman, Al Handler, Leo Kaufman, Harold London, Ed Ahern, J. Drill, and Karl Samuels – all of whom called the city of brotherly love, Philadelphia, Pennsylvania, home – expressed that "with a powerful united movement of all classes of people, regardless of their political and religious affiliations, we can – we will defeat fascism here in Spain and thus deal a deadly blow to world fascism."[226] Solomon Feldman likewise wrote to friends at the *New Masses*:

> The American boys have shown their guts, ability, willingness to give their all – to fight the terror of degradation and barbarism, so please, for the sake of the working class of the entire world, never stop for one moment in the defense of Spanish democracy, in the collecting of funds,

---

and Surgeons in 1919. He arrived in Spain June 11, 1937. He died July 7, 1960.

[225] Charley O'Flaherty, Albacete, Spain, in Marcel Acier, ed, *From Spanish Trenches: Recent Letters From Spain* (New York, Modern Age, 1937) 144. O'Flaherty, Irish American, sailed for Spain January 6, 1937, at the age of 34, aboard the *Lafayette*. He returned to the U.S. July 31, 1937 aboard the *President Roosevelt* after being wounded in action.

[226] M.H. Wickman, Al Handler, Leo Kaufman, Harold London, Ed Ahern, J. Drill, Karl Samuels in "From the Cradle of Liberty to the Tomb of Fascism: Letters from Philadelphians Fighting in Spain," (Philadelphia, The Communist Party of Eastern Pennsylvania, 1937) 4.

clearly explaining to the people the meaning of Spain.²²⁷

The German, Italian, and Portuguese governments officially backed Franco's fascist nationalists, as well as Moorish Muslim mercenaries from Morocco, which was a Spanish protectorate and one of the last vestiges of Spain's global empire that had rapidly receded after the Spanish-American war at the turn of the twentieth century. But for Italian, German, and Austrian refugees from fascism and Nazism, the Spanish War was the first chance to fight back against their oppressors back home on an actual front, rather than picket lines. In the early days of Hitler's reign, German Communists were as vilified as Jews; many thousands had been sent to concentration camps by the time the war in Spain began on July 18, 1936. The German speaking International Brigade Battalion, in fact, was named after an imprisoned German Communist leader, Ernst Thälmann.²²⁸

---

[227] Solomon Feldman in Marcel Acier, ed, *From Spanish Trenches: Recent Letters From Spain* (New York, Modern Age, 1937) 167. Acier mistakenly refers to his as "Abraham." Solomon Feldman was born September 14, 1914 in Philadelphia, Pennsylvania. He was a salesman who joined the YCL in 1935. He sailed for Spain March 17, 1937 aboard the *President Roosevelt*. He arrived in Spain May 25, 1937 after serving a forty-day sentence in a French jail for illegally trying to enter Spain aboard a small fishing boat in the Mediterranean Sea. He deserted September 15, 1937, but was listed as rehabilitated before being reported wounded in action in March 1938 in Belchite. He returned to the U.S. on October 25, 1938 aboard the *Ile de France*.

[228] Thälmann was born 16 April 1886, executed 18 August 1944.

Many of the Italian, Austrian, and German volunteers, like their American counterparts, hoped that stopping fascism in Spain would prevent it from spreading all throughout Europe, which many presciently believed would lead to another World War. Many French volunteers, the nationality that provided the largest contingent of the International Brigades, along with British and North American volunteers who went to Spain, were especially concerned about what defeat for the Spanish Republic might mean for the rest of the world. "We want peace – that's part of our job here," American volunteer, Sidney Kaufman, wrote to friends in September, 1938, just a week and a half before Spanish Premier Juan Negrín announced the expulsion of the International Brigades from Spain. "Spain is the place to smash fascism," Kaufman explained. "Should the fascists be victorious, we knew before we came here, it would only be a short time before France, England, or possibly the U.S. would be the next victim of aggression."[229]

One thing all the American volunteers whose letters survived the twentieth century seemed to share, and what drove many of them to Spain in the first place, was the notion that time was running out for the entire world, and that problems had to be met and resolved swiftly, lest the world would inevitably be dragged back into the Dark Ages by fascists and monarchists. Spain was, to many volunteers of the International Brigades, a line in the proverbial sand, which helped shape and

---

[229] Sidney Kaufman, September 12, 1938, Valencia, Spain, in Cary Nelson and Jefferson Hicks, eds. *Madrid 1937: Letters of the Abraham Lincoln Brigade From the Spanish Civil War* (New York, Routledge, 1996) 330.

mold the Republic's slogan, "No Pasaran!" (they shall not pass).

The concern for the future of the world amongst many American volunteers in the International Brigades especially manifested itself in the feelings of solidarity that they expressed in their letters gushing admiration for loyalist Spaniards. Many letters expressed genuine philia for the Spanish people. Sheldon Jones and his brother, David, both of whom served on the *U.S.S. Florida* during World War I, for instance, expressed a profound admiration for Spanish Republicans. "The people are very friendly to us and considerate in every way," Sheldon wrote his wife and son in March, 1938. "Their morale seems very good despite all attempts to terrorize them which fail. Their courage is remarkable."[230] The Jones brothers' sentimentality towards the Spanish is consonant with many other letters written by American volunteers. City College of New York student, Harry Ain, for instance, wrote to his parents: "The Spanish are a wonderful people. They have wondrous courage, and they will fight to the end to drive the fascist beasts Hitler and Mussolini from their

---

[230] Sheldon Jones in Marcel Acier, ed, *From Spanish Trenches: Recent Letters From Spain* (New York, Modern Age, 1937) 145. Sheldon Jones was born June 2, 1900 in Port Deposit, Maryland. He served aboard the *U.S.S.* Florida in World War I. He was a seamen and had no political affiliation. He sailed for Spain February 4, 1937 aboard the *Paris*, and arrived on February 14, 1937. He returned to the U.S. February 4, 1937 aboard the President Harding. He died in 1972. His brother, David, also served in Spain. Their parents had once owned a successful shoe factory, but the family fell on hard times during the Depression, which may have contributed to both men's decision to go to Spain, despite the fact that both were in their late thirties and had families.

beautiful country."[231] Leonard Levenson likewise wrote his family in 1937 that: "There is a political awareness and lust for freedom in the people that will never permit the return of the oppressors. Their method of agriculture are biblical in character but in defense of their liberty they are wielding the ultra-modern weapons of solidarity and class consciousness."[232] Bob Shissler also hailed the "gargantuan heroism of the Spanish people… a courage that will go down as one of the most magnificent things in history… determined and unconquerable spirit of the people."[233] A passage in Milton White's journal titled "Barcelona!" especially demonstrates American volunteers' sense of affection, sympathy, and solidarity for Spanish Republicans:

> Amid your ruins, your churches, your schools
> the people stand solemnly reviewing time and
> time again the excavation of their children their

---

[231] Harry Ain, June 5, 1938, ALBA vertical files, box 1, folder 9. Tamiment Library/Robert F. Wagner Labor Archives. Elmer Holmes Tamiment Library, 70 Washington Square South, New York NY 10012, New York University Libraries. Ain was born August 5, 1917 in Rockville, CT. He attended night classes at CCNY for three years while living in Brooklyn. He joined the YCL in 1933 and CP in 1935. He arrived in Spain June 22, 1937. He was killed in action in Ebro July 9, 1938.

[232] Leonard Levenson, August 30, 1937, Albacete, Spain. Levenson papers, ALBA.151, box 1, Tamiment Library/Robert F. Wagner Labor Archives. Elmer Holmes Tamiment Library, 70 Washington Square South, New York NY 10012, New York University Libraries.

[233] Bob Shissler, August 26, 1937, Soccoro Rojo, Albacete, Spain. Tamiment Library/Robert F. Wagner Labor Archives. Elmer Holmes Tamiment Library, 70 Washington Square South, New York NY 10012, New York University Libraries.

husbands their wives that have died, died suffering, in barbaric bombardments from the fascist invasion. Without a tear, but with a burning hatred against the common enemy, they stand watching. From under a pillar which had once upheld a beautiful and impressive apartment home, the unrecognizable body of a child. The people continue to look. They are not sick for they have seen this time and time again, but the expressions they have on their faces reveal what goes on in their minds. When you see a scene like this you know why it is the Spaniards will never give up but will carry on and win victoriously to remove this scene forever and ever from the face of this earth.[234]

Al Handler wrote a loved one in June, 1937 that, "We'll give them a world to live in – not a world threatened by imperialistic war, by want, privation, fear of the future. We'll fashion for them a 'bright new world.' Jesus Christ, there I go soap boxing again. But, believe me, it's honest."[235]

---

[234] Milton White, "Barcelona!" 1938. Milton White Papers, White Papers: ALBA.278, Folder, 1938 "Personal Impressions," Tamiment Library/Robert F. Wagner Labor Archives. Elmer Holmes Tamiment Library, 70 Washington Square South, New York NY 10012, New York University Libraries. White was born April 1, 1917 in Cleveland, Ohio, and attended NYU medical school from 1936-37. He was a member of the YCL as early as 1932 and made a living as a musician and actor. He arrived in Spain April 7, 1937. He was wounded in action February 2, 1938. He served in World War II. He died in New York city in June, 1983.

[235] Al Handler, June 15, 1937, Tielmas, Spain in "From the Cradle of Liberty to the Tomb of Fascism: Letters from Philadelphians Fighting in Spain," M.H. Wickman, Al

Five months earlier, in February, 1937, shortly after arriving in Spain, Bostonian, Robert Munson Taylor, likewise expressed to his friend, "Tank," how impressed he was with loyalists' courage and tenacity. "You should see some of the Spanish kids of 16 or 17 years run out (of a trench), climb up on top of a tank and heave a grenade into the peep hole," he wrote.[236] Solomon Feldman likewise regaled the courage of Spanish loyalists and noted their affection for the Americans:

> you must begin to realize the danger of fascism and war – must multiply your efforts 100 percent for Spanish democracy and for the United Front in the United States. If they are still not convinced, tell them of the eighteen-year-old young Spaniard who has been fighting since July, wounded three times, lost his brother in

---

Handler, Leo Kaufman, Harold London, Ed Ahern, J. Drill, Karl Samuels (Philadelphia, The Communist Party of Eastern Pennsylvania, 1937) 17.

[236] Robert Munson Taylor, February 25, 1937, in Marcel Acier, ed, *From Spanish Trenches: Recent Letters From Spain* (New York, Modern Age, 1937) 149. Robert Munson Taylor was born May 10, 1915 in Boston, Massachusettes. He went to Spain in January 1937 aboard the *Paris* to fight with the International Brigades in the Spanish War as a member of the Abraham Lincoln Battalion. During his time in Spain, he suffered a head injury and was at one point mistakenly reported as dead. Taylor fought in several major battles, including those in Villanueva de la Canada and Brunete. He returned August 20, 1937 aboard the *Paris*. He was living in Detroit during the summer of 1938 when the local Red Squad raided his house and held him for two days. He was accused of illegally recruiting volunteers for Spain, and a political file was kept on him for the next forty years. In 1940 he was again arrested, this time by the FBI, when crossing the Canadian border into Michigan.

action, his father and mother slaughtered at Malaga. Yet while on leave, he is taking part in war maneuvers to perfect his ability to fight fascism still more courageously and correctly. When he found we were Americans, his face beamed. Here was the great American working class come to support the Spanish people in this strife."[237]

Jack Kalleborn, an American volunteer from a family of farmers, wrote his wife, Sonia that, "Spain is doing a heroic job and doing it well in spite of all difficulties, inefficiency and sabotage within our own ranks (loyalist, including International Brigade), and shortage of supplies. But Spain must be helped, with food and medical supplies and military as well."[238] Steve Nelson, who was relentlessly persecuted as a subversive by the U.S. government in the early 1950s, measured victory not in battles won but in moral support given to the Republic. "Our greatest contribution," he said, "was

---

[237] Solomon Feldman, Marcel Acier, ed, *From Spanish Trenches: Recent Letters From Spain* (New York, Modern Age, 1937) 169.

[238] Jack Kalleborn, March 20, 1937, in Marcel Acier, ed, *From Spanish Trenches: Recent Letters From Spain* (New York, Modern Age, 1937), 171. Kalleborn was born December 21, 1909 in St. Louis, Missouri. He was a factory worker and machinist. He joined the CP in 1929. He arrived in Spain July 17, 1937 and returned February 4 aboard the President Harding. He was wounded in action. His father became and engineer but Jack ran the family farm after several years of agricultural school. He went to the Soviet Union for two years to study collective farming methods and was especially eager to know whether this system might work in the U.S. He returned home in 1934 and left for Spain toward the end of 1936.

letting the Spanish people know they were not alone."[239] George Watt similarly expressed his unwavering commitment to Spanish Republicans in a 1938 letter to his family:

> There can be no going home for anyone here until victory for Spain is guaranteed. Besides, any guy who has a chance to come to Spain and doesn't take it is losing the chance of a lifetime. The experience is worth every sacrifice even up to the highest. So tell everybody to stop writing letters to the boys here to come home as if we had some prison sentence and our time was up. Right now we can't think of home. We got enough to think about the homes in Spain. They are being destroyed by fascists. The homes in the states are still pretty safe from bombardments.[240]

The same month Canute Frankson, an African-American volunteer, expressed his affection for Spanish Republicans, writing a friend that:

> In the beginning these people had no arms with which to defend themselves and their country against their traitor rulers. But they had conviction, courage and determination…

---

[239] Steve Nelson as quoted in Noel Buckner, Mary Dore, and Sam Sills' *The Good Fight: The Abraham Lincoln Brigade in the Spanish Civil War*, 1984.

[240] George Watt to family, June 18, 1938, Barcelona, Spain. Watt Family Papers, ALBA.193, Box 1. Tamiment Library/Robert F. Wagner Labor Archives. Elmer Holmes Tamiment Library, 70 Washington Square South, New York NY 10012, New York University Libraries.

> Despite the odds against us we have some very favorable factors on our side. The people are definitely and wholeheartedly on the side of the government – because the government is for the people.[241]

A month later Frankson wrote that:

> We came because we are convinced of the cause for which they (Spanish Republicans) fight. We remain here because we could not help learning to love them. We fight with them because we know that they are representatives and defenders of freedom. We see that they represent the best in human beings: love, sympathy, tolerance, sacrifice, determination and bravery... There is in these people (Spaniards) a very evident expression of sympathy, hospitality and friendship.[242]

His admiration for them was especially pronounced because Spanish peasants shared a special kind of affection for African Americans similar to the affection black volunteers felt towards the peasantry. Despite difference in skin color, there was a profound affinity shared due to the nature of their historical oppression by nationalistic elites throughout the world. Frankson explained the shared philia between black folks and

---

[241] Canute Frankson to friend, June 26, 1937; Steve Nelson Papers, ALBA.008, Box 1, Folder, Canute Frankson Letters From Spain. Tamiment Library/Robert F. Wagner Labor Archives. Elmer Holmes Tamiment Library, 70 Washington Square South, New York NY 10012, New York University Libraries.

[242] Ibid.

Spanish peasants in an August, 1937 letter to a lover back home:

> Their (Spanish Republicans) treatment of the Negroes is something else. The only way I could possibly describe it is that it is a mixture of sympathy, affection and devotion. Sometimes I pinch myself to see if I'm dreaming. Then I realize it is no dream. But Negroes among people who represent progress. They had suffered centuries of suppression... These centuries have taught them to be conscious of the class to which they belong. And because they kept this consciousness in their minds there was no room for the racial antagonisms and hatreds so evident in our own country... These same people (the Spanish) are as hungry as we are. They live in dives and wear rags the same way we do. They, too, are robbed by their masters, and their faces kept down in the filth of a decayed system. They are our fellowmen... This, of course, is the basis for the sympathy they feel for us (African Americans) as a people... There is a picture being shown in this country. It is called *El Negro que Tiene el Alma Blanca* (The Negro With the White Soul)... Personally I do not like the title. But the result on their minds is very good. I read the story and do not like the way it was written. This Negro was a Cuban slave. But born in Madrid. He later got famous as a dancer. He got very rich. He was highly acclaimed in Paris. But he was in love with his white dancing partner. She would not return his love because of his color. And in the midst of all his fame and wealth he committed suicide. This naïve bit of propaganda, however, has won the greatest amount of sympathy of an entire nation for our people. But what impresses me most is their attitude toward us... The International Brigades, or rather the

internationals who came here to help them, are to them a symbol of international brotherhood.[243]

A month later Frankson wrote that the Spanish people were teaching the American volunteers "tolerance, sacrifice and heroism. Not that kind of heroism plastered over the pages of Hearst's paper, but a consciousness of, and a tireless resistance against, some of the greatest possible odds."[244]

The same month, Thain Summers, an American volunteer who had recently arrived at the front outside Madrid, explained:

> I see the way the people's government of Spain is operating as an expression of the people and fulfilling the needs of the people in the most inevitable way, from the fundamental necessities of food up to the needs of education, culture and art. I cannot help but see the tremendous contrast between the spontaneity, initiative and brotherliness of the whole society here in Spain, as contrasted with the class distinctions and hatreds in the U.S., in spite of their greater wealth.[245]

---

[243] Ibid.

[244] Ibid.

[245] Thain Summers, November 28, 1937, ALBA Vertical Files, box 8, folder 53, Tamiment Library/Robert F. Wagner Labor Archives. Elmer Holmes Tamiment Library, 70 Washington Square South, New York NY 10012, New York University Libraries. Summers was born March 24, 1914 in Seattle Washington and was a graduate of the University of

The mutual admiration and devotion between the American volunteers and Spanish Republicans did not go unnoticed by war correspondent Martha Gellhorn, who in April, 1938, likewise expressed her solidarity and affection for both in a letter to her friend, Eleanor Roosevelt.

> Franco will have to do away with about twenty million Spaniards before he could ever rule this country... I find myself foolishly patriotic about the Americans – about half the Lincoln-Washington Battalion is lost since the last push – I find I love them immeasurably, am immeasurably proud of them, individually and collectively, and proud of their record and proud of the reasons that brought them here and keep them here. I never saw better men in my life in any country, and what they are willing to die for if need be is what you – in your way and place – are willing to live for."[246]

Many letters also allude to a deep sense of brotherhood amongst Spaniards towards the American volunteers. "Whenever the International Brigade travels in Spain, the Spanish people are enthusiastic about us," John Field wrote. "I have ridden through orange groves of Valencia and have had bushels of oranges thrown in the train; Through Madeira and have had bushels of

---

Washington. He was a CP member. He arrived in Spain June 2, 1937 and was killed in action in Belchite in March 1938.

[246] Martha Gellhorn wrote to Eleanor Roosevelt, April 24 and 25, 1938, Barcelona, Spain, Box 1459, Franklin D. Roosevelt Library, Hyde Park, New York

grapes thrown in."[247] George Watt similarly hailed Spaniard's generosity in a letter to a friend, "Peasants fed us nuts and oranges. The Spanish are wonderfully generous and hospitable." [248] A Columbia University-trained historian and economist, Paul Wendorf, also noted the affection of Spanish Republicans towards American volunteers in 1938 letter to his wife. "The peasants came out carrying jugs of wine and water, glad to see us, glad to know that all the people in Barcelona haven't been killed, as the fascists had told them." Theodor Veltfort wrote in October, 1937, "When I was in Valencia once to get a load of meat the Spanish 'responsible' invited me to his home to have supper and to stay for the night. It was the very modest quarters of a worker's family but they dug up a real meal in honor of the visiting Norteamericano [sic]."[249] Robert Munson

---

[247] John Field, SRI, Plaza del Altozano, Albacete, Spain October 9, 1937, ALBA vertical files, box 2, folder 145, Tamiment Library/Robert F. Wagner Labor Archives. Elmer Holmes Tamiment Library, 70 Washington Square South, New York NY 10012, New York University Libraries.

[248] George Watt to Terry, May 5, 1938, Barcelona, Spain. Watt Family Papers, ALBA.193, Box 1, Tamiment Library/Robert F. Wagner Labor Archives. Elmer Holmes Tamiment Library, 70 Washington Square South, New York NY 10012, New York University Libraries. George Watt, aka Israel Kwatt, was born November 5, 1913 in New York City. He attended Brooklyn College and Cooper Union Institute of Technology. He was a member of the YCL in 1932 and CP in 1937. He sailed for Spain aboard the *Britannic* and arrived in Spain August 9, 1937. He was wounded in action October 13, 1937 at Fuentes de Ebro. He was promoted is Commissar April 8, 1938. He returned to the U.S. aboard the *Ausonia* December 20, 1938. He was a crewmember on a bomber during WWII, and died July 1994 in Northport, Rhode Island.

[249] Theodor Veltfort, October 16, 1937, Aragon Front, ALBA Vertical Files, box 8, folder 109. Tamiment

Taylor similarly gushed that "The women treat us well and they do a million and one things for us such as washing, sewing, etc."[250] Joe Dallet wrote his wife that, "Next to the Red pilots – who are national heroes here, our boys get probably more praise than any others."[251] Ernest Amatniek, a scientist from City College of New York, also wrote about the comradeship between Spaniards and the American volunteers from a hospital where he was recovering from a shrapnel wound to his leg. "There is a kid teaching me Spanish – by talking to me," he explained to a friend back home. "The most popular subject is movies, then politics; he is an Anarchist. He can walk around, so buys me anything I need."[252]

Library/Robert F. Wagner Labor Archives. Elmer Holmes Tamiment Library, 70 Washington Square South, New York NY 10012, New York University Libraries. Veltfort was born February 29, 1915 in Cambridge, Massachusetts. He attended Princeton and Swarthmore. He was a member of the YCL and CP in Connecticut. He arrived in Spain July 4, 1937, and served as a truck and ambulance driver. He returned to the U.S. December 20, 1938 aboard the *Ausonia*. He also served in WWII. He died in Oakland, California, April 7, 2008.

[250] Robert Munson Taylor, February 25, 1937, in Marcel Acier, ed, *From Spanish Trenches: Recent Letters From Spain* (New York, Modern Age, 1937) 149.

[251] Joe Dallet, Albacete, Spain, May 3, 1937 "Letters From Spain, American Volunteer to His Wife" (New York, Workers Library Publishers, 1938), 35. ALBA vertical files, box 2, folder 60. Tamiment Library/Robert F. Wagner Labor Archives. Elmer Holmes Tamiment Library, 70 Washington Square South, New York NY 10012, New York University Libraries.

[252] Ernest Amatniek, November 1, 1937, A hospital on Terrasona, Spain, ALBA vertical files, box 1, folder 21. Tamiment Library/Robert F. Wagner Labor Archives. Elmer

Amatniek's affection with a Spanish Anarchist is especially instructive because the official Communist party line by the time he penned the letter was a devout demonization of Anarchists, who were falsely accused by Stalin of being Trotskyist agents for Franco. Amatniek's affection for the Spanish Anarchist demonstrates the fact that the American volunteers, even card-carrying members of the Communist Party such as Amatniek, were not Stalinist automatons; they were, above all, idealists guided by a deep sense of brotherly love for humanity, especially Spanish Republicans.

But the longer the American volunteers were in Spain the more bitterly frustrated with the U.S. government many of them became. The most "disgraceful part is the failure of the democratic nations to help the suffering Spanish people, who are making all these sacrifices, heroically and willingly, for the peace and democracy of the world," Carl Geiser fumed in December, 1937.[253] But despite frustration with their government, many volunteers were proud Americans who regretted that their political leaders were increasingly abandoning the ideals that had originally caused the U.S. to revolt against the British Empire in the eighteenth century. A month before receiving

---

Holmes Tamiment Library, 70 Washington Square South, New York NY 10012, New York University Libraries.

[253] Carl Geiser to Bea December 19, 1937; Carl Geiser Papers, ALBA.004, folder: Outgoing Correspondence, April – May 1937; Tamiment Library/Robert F. Wagner Labor Archives. Elmer Holmes Tamiment Library, 70 Washington Square South, New York NY 10012, New York University Libraries.

Geiser's letter, his wife, Sylvia, sent a birthday invitation to friends urging them to come over to their apartment and celebrate Carl's birthday by reading his letters. The invitation described her husband as "an American farm boy carrying forward the traditions of true Americanism."[254] The description underscores the fact that many American volunteers viewed themselves to be fighting for values central to the American Revolution.

For the Greek philosopher Aristotle, in order to feel the highest form of philia for another, one must first feel it for oneself. While many of the Americans' letters home consistently express a fraternity and affinity for Spanish loyalists, who they perceived to be part of the globally oppressed working class of the world, their letters especially evoke a philia for other Americans and their homeland. Many American volunteers' unabashed identification of themselves as members of the world's working class was not mutually exclusive from self-identification as patriotic Americans. In fact, many Americans perceived themselves to be carrying on the radical tradition established in the 1760s and 1770s as the U.S. broke away from the British Empire.

Harry Ain, for instance, evoked the spirit of the American Revolution in a letter to his parents, writing "I hope the United States will soon repeal her so called 'neutrality' law and help a sister democracy which is

---

[254] Birthday invitation, November 20, 1937. Carl Geiser Papers, ALBA.004, folder: Outgoing Correspondence, 1937. Tamiment Library/Robert F. Wagner Labor Archives. Elmer Holmes Tamiment Library, 70 Washington Square South, New York NY 10012, New York University Libraries.

fighting the same battle the U.S. was fighting in 1776."[255] A similar sentiment was expressed by Dartmouth grad turned union organizer, Joe Dallet, in May, 1937:

> The U.S. continues to disgrace itself by selling large quantities of supplies used in making ammunition to Germany and Italy, while refusing any kind of assistance to the democratic, friendly and legally elected government of Spain. What a far cry from the days of 1776! What a blot upon the pages of American History! What a fateful policy for a democratic country, itself menaced by pro-fascist forces from within, to pursue in the face of the infamous, brutal actions of international fascism![256]

Soon after returning to the U.S. from his tour of duty in Spain, Norman Dorland expressed his patriotism in a letter to schoolmates in Memphis, Tennessee, in which he tried to appeal to their sense of history and nationalism to win support for the Spanish Republic:

> As the people of our country are beginning to see the role of the American volunteers who

---

[255] Harry Ain to parents June 5, 1938, ALBA vertical files, box 1, folder 9. Tamiment Library/Robert F. Wagner Labor Archives. Elmer Holmes Tamiment Library, 70 Washington Square South, New York NY 10012, New York University Libraries.

[256] Joe Dallet, May 31, 1937, Albacete, Spain, Joe Dallet Papers, ALBA.032, Box 1, folder: 1937; Tamiment Library/Robert F. Wagner Labor Archives. Elmer Holmes Tamiment Library, 70 Washington Square South, New York NY 10012, New York University Libraries.

fought for the liberty of the Spanish people against Hitler's, Mussolini's and Franco's troops, and as two-thirds of these fine men have paid the supreme sacrifice of giving their lives to stop fascism, in the best and truest spirit of American traditions of Democracy, Liberty and the Pursuit of Happiness – we can best honor them by placing them alongside our fathers and brothers who fought in France (in World War I), with the full realization that they also understood clearly and answered quickly to the need of an oppressed people.[257]

What is especially instructive in many American volunteers' letters is how central their American identity and sense of history was to their willingness to risk life, limb, and citizenship by fighting in Spain. In March, 1938, for instance, Sheldon Jones wrote, "I came here because I thought that as an American it was my duty to support, to the best of my ability, a people struggling for their elementary rights and freedom from age-old

---

[257] Norman Dorland, December 9, 1938; Steve Nelson Papers, ALBA.008, Box 4, Folder "Spanish Civil War Memoirs;" Tamiment Library/Robert F. Wagner Labor Archives. Elmer Holmes Tamiment Library, 70 Washington Square South, New York NY 10012, New York University Libraries. Dorland was born July 5, 1912 in St. Paul Minnesota. He was an engineer, seaman and member of the CP in 1936. He sailed for Spain aboard the *President Roosevelt*, and arrived in Spain May 15, 1937. He was captured by Nationalist forces March 12, 1938 at Lecera and exchanged October 8, 1938. He returned to the U.S. on October 18, 1938 aboard the *Queen Mary*. He served as a Merchant Marine in WWII and was awarded three decorations. He died in July 1964 in an auto accident.

oppression."[258] A month later, in April, 1938, Sheldon's brother, David, wrote a loved one back home that Spain was "going to be the world's second greatest country (after the U.S.)."[259] Very many American volunteers, as the Jones brothers' sentiment helps illuminate, were very proud Americans who expressed a genuine affection for their homeland and concern for its future. As much as the American volunteers expressed fraternity for workers of the world and Spanish loyalists, they especially expressed sentiments of fraternity and brotherly love for Americans and the U.S. writ large, which they feared was being dragged into another World War by Hitler, Mussolini, and Franco, all of whom benefited from British, French, and American official neutrality. In May, 1937, for instance, Carl Geiser wrote that:

> The reasons I am here is because I want to do my part to prevent a second world war, which would without doubt, draw in the United States and seriously set back our civilization. And secondly, because all of our democratic and liberty-loving training makes me anxious to fight fascism, and to help the Spanish people drive out the fascist invaders sent in by Hitler &

---

[258] Sheldon Jones, March 8, 1938, in Marcel Acier, ed, *From Spanish Trenches: Recent Letters From Spain* (New York, Modern Age, 1937) 146.

[259] David Jones, April 21, 1937, Marcel Acier, ed, *From Spanish Trenches: Recent Letters From Spain* (New York, Modern Age, 1937) 146. Jones was a Boston resident and member of the CP as early as 1925. He sailed for Spain aboard the *Lafayette* January 9, 1937 at the age of 39. He served as a Commissar in Spain. He was wounded in action April 15, 1937. His brother, Sheldon, also served with the Lincoln Battalion.

> Mussolini… So you can see, it is a matter of checking fascism and war, of preserving democracy & peace. We ought not think that if the fascists take Spain we are safe, no more than we ought to think our house is safe if the neighbor's is on fire. Protect yours by helping your neighbor put out his fire. That is why the idea of "neutrality," of keeping out of Spain, is very wrong and harmful. Everyone who wants democracy and peace must help the Spanish government, and right away. Frankly, if the Spanish government is victorious, Germany & Italy will be surrounded by more or less democratic countries, and we shall have an excellent chance of avoiding another world war.[260]

In a 1939 radio speech made shortly after he returned from Spain, George Watt pleaded with Americans to support the Republic's enduring yet fledgling fight against fascism:

> Spaniards, like Americans, would choose to die for their liberty rather than live as slaves under foreign invaders… The costly sacrifices which Spain is making now are minute in comparison to the destruction of human lives and property which will follow in a world war if Spain loses. Many Spaniards knowing that I was American have told me that the American people will

---

[260] Carl Geiser, May 9, 1937, Albacete, Spain; ALBA vertical files, box 3, folder 41. Tamiment Library/Robert F. Wagner Labor Archives. Elmer Holmes Tamiment Library, 70 Washington Square South, New York NY 10012, New York University Libraries.

realize that Spain is fighting not only for its own independence but also to save all world democracies from fascist aggression. Spain is still the first line of resistance against the planned offensive directed at all democratic countries. The longer Spain resists, the more time and hope there is for the people of the world to gather their collective power to preserve our democracies.[261]

Even some outlets of the popular press in the U.S. expressed the fact that the volunteers were, above all else, proud Americans. "You cannot dismiss these youngsters with the contemptuous label of 'reds,' *New York Times* Madrid correspondent Herbert Matthews wrote in 1937. He added:

> They are not fighting for Moscow, but for their ideals and because they would rather die than see a fascist regime under any shape or auspices installed in the United States. The American battalions are unique in one respect; among all the Internationals they remain American to the core. None of the internationals are so conscious of their nationality… In the overalls that are the uniform of those who fight for the Spanish Republic, they are readily recognized as boys from home: 'Yankees.' They come from every walk of life: among them there are steelworkers

---

[261] George Watt, Radio Speech, 1939 (attempt to garner aid and material for Spain), Watt Family Papers: ALBA.193. Tamiment Library/Robert F. Wagner Labor Archives. Elmer Holmes Tamiment Library, 70 Washington Square South, New York NY 10012, New York University Libraries.

and artists, furriers and schoolteachers. Their battalion carries the name of Abraham Lincoln.[262]

The same sentiment was also expressed in more leftist publications, such as a 1937 article titled, "From the Cradle of Liberty to the Tomb of Fascism: Letters from Philadelphians Fighting in Spain," which was printed by The Communist Party of Eastern Pennsylvania:

> You will soon celebrate July 4th, Independence Day, which symbolizes the freedom of the American people from British tyranny. In that fight, our ancestors were not alone. Thousands of people came across the Atlantic and died for our country. We are proud of people like Lafayette and Kosciusko, foreigners who helped Americans to defeat the British. We Philadelphians, together with other hundreds of Americans who cherish Liberty, are carrying out the same mission here in the front lines, giving out help to the Spanish people in their fight for independence from the murderous barbarism of invading fascism… (Many of) our comrades of the Lincoln Battalion have given their lives on the battlefield in order that democracy might live. Those brave heroes are the symbol of Americanism and the true sons of America.[263]

---

[262] April 25, 1937, *The New York Times* in Herbert Matthews, *Two Wars and More to Come*, (New York, Carrick & Evans, 1938) 220.

[263] M.H. Wickman, Al Handler, Leo Kaufman, Harold London, Ed Ahern, J. Drill, Karl Samuels, "From the Cradle of

The *Southern Worker,* which interviewed two parents from Alabama whose son had joined the Lincolns in 1937, expressed a similar patriotism as a motive for going to Spain:

> One of my great great grandfathers fought in Washington's army in New York during the Revolutionary War. Some of his sons fought in the Civil War. I know I've fought all my life, and my father before me. We've fought for all the things especially dear to Americans, the things that the Constitution is supposed to guarantee us. My great great grandfather was an artisan who came over from Ireland. And in the war for independence he gave his life not only to break the chains that held us under the tyranny of the English Empire, but to set up in this beautiful country of ours a government and set of laws that would let every man say what he pleased, come together and discuss what he wanted to, and print it for others to read... Early in my father's life he found that he did not actually have the things for which our ancestors had fought. A ruling class had grown up in America, which owned everything. There were no strong workers' organizations... The bosses then as today paid the lowest wages they could get away with. The banks robbed him of his land when he tried to farm. Towards the end of the century, my father realized that the only way that he and people like him were ever going to

---

Liberty to the Tomb of Fascism: Letters from Philadelphians Fighting in Spain," (Philadelphia, The Communist Party of Eastern Pennsylvania, 1937) 3-4.

have any real security and freedom would be for all the people who were stepped on and exploited to build a new world – a socialist world where there wouldn't be any ruling class.[264]

Very many American volunteers – regardless of their political persuasions, class, race, ethnicity or gender – had American Dreams and wanted to see them fulfilled. But the overwhelming economic crisis of the 1930s made the American Dream, so closely associated with social mobility, seem increasingly unattainable. These young people, many of whom came of age in the Roaring Twenties or Great Depression, were, despite economic calamity and social despair, deeply idealistic and hopeful that stopping fascism in Spain would make their own nation safer and more prosperous. The fascism many believed was pulling the world back towards the Dark Ages threatened the very fabric of the values many of them associated with the American way of life.

As such, as much as American volunteers' letters expressed affection for their homeland, they concomitantly expressed grave concern for the nation's future. By August, 1941, just a few months before Japan bombed Pearl Harbor, Lincoln vet Albert Prago evoked American history and sounded a clarion call in an

---

[264] Mr. Williams' father was a lumberjack, and then a coal miner and iron worker. Pat Barr, "Mary and I are Glad Our Son Went to Spain: Southern Father and Mother Tell Us How the Spanish People's Fight For Democracy Belongs to Them" *Southern Worker: Magazine of the Common Worker of the South* Vol. V, No. 16. Chattanooga, Tenn. July 1937, p. 8

attempt to provoke political readers to be wary of the fascism already within the U.S.:

> The period of the epoch-making American Revolutionary War saw its Benedict Arnolds and Tories; Jeffersonian Democracy during the War of 1812 was faced with the treachery of the Federalists who, like the Tories, remain only as historical blots on the glorious records of those progressives like Franklin and Jefferson whose ideals still live. Today, in the universal struggle against fascism, we are confronted by the Quislings. We warn the American people against ex-Col. Charles A. Lindbergh, Herbert Hoover, Senator Wheeler, Norman Thomas and their like for they are the Quislings of America. As did Quisling in Norway, and Laval and Petain in France, the Lindbergh-Hoover outfit would bring Hitlerism to America.[265]

Fear of fascists starting another world war was a pervasive theme in American volunteers' letters during the Spanish War. "I don't want America in a war – I know what it means," Leonard Levenson wrote to a couple of buddies in November, 1937 hoping to win their support for the Republic. "But I know just as surely that the only way out for her is to join with the Soviet Union in an active fight for peace. Don't let it merely be

---

[265] Albert Prago, *We Fought Hitler* (New York, Veterans of the Abraham Lincoln Brigade, August 1941) 9. Prago's proverbial shot across the bow in which he calls J. Edgar Hoover a fascist helps illuminate why the FBI so religiously and mercilessly attacked the Lincolns during the Cold War.

the same old story of the Morgans and Mellons deciding when, where, and with whom."[266]

Ten days after Levenson wrote his buddies, Hyman Katz wrote his mother that, "Together with their agent, Franco, they (Hitler and Mussolini) are trying to set up the same anti-progressive, anti-Semitic regime in Spain, as they have in Italy and Germany. If we sit by and let them grow stronger by taking Spain, they will move onto France and will not stop there; and it won't be long before they get to America."[267] Eugene Wolman expressed a similar sentiment to his father in March, 1938. "Unless these forces are stopped," he wrote, "we are sure to have another war."[268] A month later, William Sennett wrote his friend, Gussie, from the Aragon Front that:

> More and more developments here and in the world hit closer home to America. How the false policy of neutrality can continue under present conditions is beyond me. If Hitler and Mussolini win here, they will go after bigger game, which will bring a new world war in its wake.

---

[266] Leonard Levenson, November 15, 1937, Madrid, in Cary Nelson and Jefferson Hicks, eds. *Madrid 1937: Letters of the Abraham Lincoln Brigade From the Spanish Civil War* (New York, Routledge, 1996) 317.

[267] Hyman Katz, November 25, 1937, Albacete, Spain, Cary Nelson and Jefferson Hicks, eds. *Madrid 1937: Letters of the Abraham Lincoln Brigade From the Spanish Civil War* (New York, Routledge, 1996) 32.

[268] Eugene Wolman, March 13, 1938, Los Angeles California, in Cary Nelson and Jefferson Hicks, eds. *Madrid 1937: Letters of the Abraham Lincoln Brigade From the Spanish Civil War* (New York, Routledge, 1996) 30.

> Economically and politically America is definitely a leading factor in world affairs and only the naïve would think that she can stay out of a new world war.[269]

Of course, history proved the American volunteers correct about fascism and American neutrality paving the way for another world war, which ultimately cost tens of millions of people lives and subsequently set the stage for the Cold War and a half-century of numerous American interventions in military conflicts around the globe, namely the Vietnam War.

What ultimately enabled the Spanish Nationalists' rebellion to continue and ultimately succeed in wresting power from the democratically elected Popular Front government was the conspicuous intercession of other European empires and the U.S.[270] By their dithering non-intervention policies to overwhelming fascist aggression in Spain, the Western democracies gave Hitler all the proof he needed that further aggression would go unchecked. For the Axis Powers, victory over the Spanish Republic was, as many American volunteers warned, tantamount to being given a key to Europe. British Prime Minister Neville Chamberlain's appeasement of Hitler in Munich provoked a startled response in the U.S., a "return to sanity," as it were, by certain American policymakers.

---

[269] William Sennett, April 16, 1938, Aragon Front, Spain, Cary Nelson and Jefferson Hicks, eds. *Madrid 1937: Letters of the Abraham Lincoln Brigade From the Spanish Civil War* (New York, Routledge, 1996) 325.

[270] James Neugrass, introduction by Peter Carroll, *War is Beautiful: An American Ambulance Driver in the Spanish Civil War*, (New York, The New Press, 2008) xii.

Even Under Secretary of State Sumner Welles lamented that, "of all our blind isolationist policies, the most disastrous was our attitude on the Spanish Civil War."[271] But by then, World War II was inevitable. Perhaps most odd of all, despite the volunteers' prophetic wisdom – or perhaps because of it – many of them were, upon returning home from Spain, assailed for their "disloyalty" to the country so many of the Lincolns expressed such genuine devotion and fraternity to and for during the Spanish War.

---

[271] Sumner Welles, *The Time For Decision*, p. 57.

Epilogue

Charles Edward Coughlin, better known as Father Coughlin, was an especially vociferous critic of American volunteers for the Spanish Republic. He was a controversial Roman Catholic priest based near Detroit, Michigan, and one of the first political leaders to exploit the radio to reach a mass audience; as many as thirty million listeners tuned in to his weekly broadcasts during the 1930s. After the 1936 presidential election, Coughlin falsely accused President Franklin Roosevelt of "leaning toward international socialism on the Spanish question" and increasingly perpetuated the notion that Adolf Hitler, Benito Mussolini and Francisco Franco's brand of fascism was a far lesser evil than communism.[272] He also claimed that Jewish bankers were behind the Russian Revolution, and that Russian Bolshevism was largely a Jewish conspiracy to subvert Christianity around the world.[273] He also charged the American members of the International Brigades, nearly forty percent of whom had Jewish roots, with "fighting for the hammer and sickle."[274] The Federal Bureau of Investigation's J. Edgar Hoover

---

[272] Sheldon Marcus, *Father Coughlin: The Tumultuous Life Of The Priest Of The Little Flower* (Boston, Little, Brown and Co. 1972) 189 – 190.

[273] Marcus, *Father Coughlin: The Tumultuous Life Of The Priest Of The Little Flower* (Boston, Little, Brown and Co. 1972) 188, 189, 190, 256 188-189; and Charles J. Tull, *Father Coughlin and the New Deal* (Syracuse, N.Y.: Syracuse University Press, 1965) 197;

[274] Coughlin as quoted in as quoted in Noel Buckner, Mary Dore, and Sam Sills' *The Good Fight: The Abraham Lincoln Brigade in the Spanish Civil War*, 1984.

likewise argued that American volunteers who went to Spain "furthered Bolshevism's international greed."[275]

From the 1930s through 1980s many conservatives labeled American volunteers as "subversives," "traitors," "Reds," "premature anti-fascists" and/or "automatons" or "dupes" who "fought for the hammer and sickle" and/or for Stalin's totalitarian brand of communism.

But Stalin neither nor the Soviet Union were hardly ever mentioned in American volunteers' letters, especially compared to the language of liberty, equality and fraternity that was especially prevalent in their discourse. When Soviet leadership was mentioned in American volunteers' correspondence, it, at least the bits overlooked by censors, was more often in criticism than praise. Despite criticism by archconservatives such as Coughlin and Hoover, eighty-seven percent of Americans in the 1930s favored the Spanish Republic in war against the fascists, which helps demonstrate how un-subversive the American volunteers actually were in contrast to the thirteen percent, such as Coughlin and Hoover, who did not quite hope for the restoration of the Republic of Spain's democratically elected Popular Front Government.[276]

Despite the prevalence of idealism, namely liberty, equality and fraternity, expressed in American

---

[275] Allen Guttmann, *The Wound in the Heart: America and the Spanish Civil War* (New York, The Free Press/Macmillan, 1962) 2.

[276] Eric Hobsbawm, "War of Ideas," *The Guardian*, February 17, 2007.

volunteers' letters, by the time the U.S. dropped atomic bombs on Japan, many had already been "suspected of disloyalty" by American conservatives and as subversive to national values, which compels one to wonder: what exactly were American values in the decades after World War II? Were they more fascistic than idealistic? Allen Guttmann pondered this very question in his 1962 classic, *The Wound in the Heart: America and the Spanish Civil War*: "Most of the Americans who supported the Republic seem more American than the officials who have questioned their loyalty," he wrote. "One sometimes feels that the men who named their volunteer unit 'The Abraham Lincoln Battalion' were closer to the traditions of liberal democracy than are the men who persistently include General Franco's Nuevo Estado within the limits of that oddly gerrymandered jurisdiction, 'The Free World.'"[277]

Despite pride in being some of the first Americans to fight Hitler's brand of fascism in Spain in 1937-38, which many volunteers believed was rooted in their love for their own country and the ideals they believed it historically stood for, many were treated as enemies of state as a result of acting on the idealism that compelled them to go Spain. To be violently opposed to anti-fascism during WWII was widely considered to be righteous; but being an anti-fascist during the Spanish War was, ironically, during the early years of the Cold War, equated by some conservatives with being "guilty of an excessive fervency" that was considered

---

[277] Allen Guttmann, *The Wound in the Heart: America and the Spanish Civil War* (New York, The Free Press/Macmillan, 1962) 213.

synonymous with "anti-Americanism."[278] But those who went to Spain to fight Franco in the hope of staving off World War II, despite their demonization by conservatives such as Martin Dies, J. Edgar Hoover and Ronald Reagan during the Cold War, "never minded being called 'pre-mature anti-fascists,'" Alvah Bessie wrote. Many American volunteers, such as Bessie – who was blacklisted as a member of the Hollywood Ten – "were proud of the label."[279]

Ironically, within five years after each letter studied in this project, the U.S. was officially a "gallant ally" with the Soviet Union in World War II against the Axis Powers – Germany, Italy and Japan.[280] But by 1947, when Franco proclaimed the restoration of the monarchy in Spain, the Soviets were the U.S.'s greatest enemy in a seemingly endless Cold War in which reason was increasingly subsumed by paranoia.[281] Part of the reason for such vociferous ferocity and

---

[278] Cecil Eby, *Between the Bullet and the Lie: American Volunteers in the Spanish Civil War*, (San Francisco, Holt, Rhinehart and Winston, 1969) 315.

[279] Alvah Bessie, *Men in Battle: A Story of Americans in Spain*, (New York, Scribner, 1939).

[280] Hugh M. Jenkins, "Free For All," *The Washington Post*, May 31, 1997, A.17.

[281] Despite restoration of the monarchy the Generalissimo remained a quasi-Rey with absolute power in Spain until his death in 1975. The irony of the Nationalist coup comprised of monarchists, the Catholic Clergy, and industrialists together with military elites was that the monarchy's power was not really restored beyond that of a nostalgic figurehead. Fascism simply took the place of monarchy.

paranoia to communism during the Cold War was the fact that in the 1950s, Franco became an ally with the United States, which means those who fought against him in the 1930s were de facto enemies of the postwar American Empire. The U.S. sponsored the "Pact of Madrid" in 1953, which subsidized Franco's dictatorship with more than two billion dollars in annual military and economic aid in exchange for American naval and air bases on Spanish soil. And in 1955, Germany and Italy were granted membership in the United Nations.[282]

---

[282] Arthur H. Landis, *The Abraham Lincoln Brigade* (New York, Citadel Press, 1967) 599. Landis was born into a family of vaudeville performers in Birmingham, Alabama in 1917, and spent most of his youth in Redondo Beach, California. During the Depression, Landis moved across the Western states picking up work in canneries, mills, and on fruit farms. In April 1937, at 19, Landis went to Spain to fight in the Spanish Civil War. He worked as a scout, a typographer, and an artillery spotter with the MacKenzie-Papineau Battalion, and fought in the battles of Aragon and Teruel, where he was injured. Landis also worked for a stint for an intelligence unit, and participated in an aborted operation to blow up the Italian Fleet headquarters. Just before Barcelona fell to Franco, Landis helped load the 15th Brigade Archives onto a Soviet ship. He sailed back to the U.S. on the *R.M.S. Ausonia* in December 1938. Shortly after his return to the U.S., Landis married Ruth Jurow, and went to work for her father as a ladies clothing salesman in Rochester, Minnesota. Struggling financially, Landis and Jurow moved to Mexico City before settling in California in 1944. Landis and Jurow later divorced. It was in the mid-1950s that Landis began to actively pursue a career as a writer. In 1967 Landis published The Abraham Lincoln Brigade, an account of the experiences of Americans who fought in the Spanish Civil War. The book was based largely upon the reminiscences of SCW veterans, which Landis collected via correspondence and on audiotapes (the latter comprise of the Arthur H. Landis Audiotape Collection). The year his book came out, Landis was awarded a medal by the Presidium of the Soviet Committee of War-Veterans for his "great contribution in the history of the struggle of the Internationalists against fascism on the battlefields of Spain."

The more important Germany, Italy, Japan and Spain became to the U.S. in military terms and as trade partners, and as bulwarks against the threat of communism, the more ardently the American volunteers for the Republic of Spain were vilified by fascists within the U.S. state department and mass media.

By the 1960s the American empire and its military industrial complex was backing anti-democratic fascist dictators around the globe including Vietnam, Greece (the former cradle of democracy), as well as Franco's Spain, prompting *The New York Times* to denounce President Dwight Eisenhower for interrupting his summer activities to congratulate Franco on the "happy anniversary of his rebellion." Two years after Ike's salutation to Franco, *The Times* likewise lamented President John F. Kennedy's secretary of state paying tribute to Spain's dictator. John Davis Lodge, an ambassador to Spain, replied with a lengthy rebuttal to *The Times'* criticism of U.S. sponsorship of Franco's regime, arguing that Spain especially understood "the implacable nature of the communist threat." Carlton

---

In 1972, Landis published Spain! The Unfinished Revolution, about the political complexities on the Republican side of the Spanish Civil War. The book was published by Camelot, a company run by Landis with close friend and fellow SCW veteran, Manny Harriman. Despite a bitter dispute with the leadership of the Volunteers of the Abraham Lincoln Brigade (VALB) in the mid-1970s over the unauthorized translation into Russian of an essay written by Landis, Landis remained devoted to VALB throughout his life, contributing occasional articles to the association's newsletter, *The Volunteer*, and maintaining close associations with many VALB members. In addition to his political writing and radical activism (he participated in the anti-Vietnam War movement in the 1960s, among other activities), Landis established himself as a fantasy and science fiction writer.

Hayes, a historian and onetime ambassador to Franco's Spain in the 1950s said, "The central significance of the Spanish Civil War was its rescue of Spain from the fate which later befell the nations of eastern Europe... the Spanish struggle," he said, "was a prelude not so much to the second World War as to the subsequent Cold War and struggle in Korea."[283]

By the time of Ronald Reagan's ascendance as President of the United States in 1981 – fewer than six years after Franco's reign finally ended as a result of his death – Catalonia and the Basque country were granted home rule (to a modest degree), but both regions were still seeking the total independence they had waged war for in the 1930s. By the fall of the Berlin Wall in 1989, unemployment in Spain ran as high as sixteen to twenty percent, which was comparable to the Great Depression, and as bad as economies throughout Eastern Europe. Although Spain had developed a thriving tourism industry during the Franco regime that attracted well-to-do leisure seekers from around the globe, including the U.S., England, France, Italy and Germany, Spain's economy was largely dependent on U.S. trade agreements for subsistence.[284] This fact helps explain why the American volunteers' idealism was so erroneously debased by conservative cynics in the decades after the 1930s. Many critics, such as Hoover and Reagan, often exhibited a greater affinity towards

---

[283] Allen Guttmann, *The Wound in the Heart: America and the Spanish Civil War* (New York, The Free Press/Macmillan, 1962) 2.

[284] Don Lawson, *The Abraham Lincoln Brigade: Americans Fighting Fascism in the Spanish Civil War* (New York, Thomas Y. Crowell, 1989) 136-137.

fascism than for liberty, equality, and fraternity for the proverbial "people" of the world, especially the anti-colonial "Third World," as well as African-Americans.

Perhaps the most ironic thing regarding the American volunteers' sense of liberty, equality and fraternity was, as Guttmann alluded to, the fact that, although Hitler and Mussolini's brand of fascism was finally checked in no small measure by U.S. intervention in World War II, fascism, as the Dies Committee, McCarthyism, and postwar militarism makes glaringly apparent, had made serious inroads into American domestic and foreign policy in the decades after World War II, which is not surprising considering the former Axis Powers became crucial trade partners with the U.S. during the Cold War. The U.S. had rapidly gone from dogmatically isolationism during the Interwar Era to the antithesis of isolationism in a matter of a generation. Thus, it was inevitable that the U.S. would become as much of the world as the world had become of the U.S.

But the sea change in American foreign policy from isolationist to military supremacy (in terms of money spent) during the Cold War further obscured the reasons many Americans were willing to risk life, limb, and citizenship to fight the same brand of fascism in Spain in 1937-38 as that which the U.S. was forced to wage war against from 1941-1945. Although eighty percent of Americans wanted the Republic of Spain to beat Hitler, Mussolini, and Franco's fascists in the 1930s, by the start of the Cold War the American volunteers' idealism prominently expressed in their letters home to friends and family had been reduced and debauched to "Bolshevism" by demagogues within the U.S. state department.

Nearly fifty years after Father Coughlin reduced the volunteers' motives for going to Spain to them fighting for the "hammer and sickle," another demagogue, President Reagan, in 1984, likewise said, with no irony whatsoever, that Americans who fought for the Spanish Republic had fought on the "wrong side."[285] In his eagerness to engage in Cold War-Culture War rhetoric Reagan was likely too confused or ignorant of history to realize he was indicating that fighting for Franco's fascist rebels, who were heavily aided by Hitler and Mussolini, was the proverbial "right side" of the fight in contrast to the American volunteers' service to the democratically elected Republican government. In Reagan's defense, many American volunteers for the Spanish Republic were associated with Popular Front organizations during the Great Depression, but that should not serve as an indication that they had fought for Stalin, the Soviet Union, or Bolshevism. It should, in fact, indicate a degree of idealism increasingly uncommon by the 1980s "greed is good" era of individualism increasingly dominant in American popular culture, especially political culture, during the waning decades of what Henry Luce referred to as "the American Century."

Coughlin, Hoover, and Reagan's insinuations that the American volunteers who went to Spain went to spread Bolshevism ultimately underscore the myriad ways in which more than a half-century of Cold War cynicism and Culture War rhetoric, designed to demonize liberalism, obscured the idealism behind many of the Americans' motives for risking life, limb,

---

[285] "Remark by Reagan on Lincoln Brigade Prompts Ire in Spain," *New York Times*, May 10, 1985, A11.

citizenship, jobs and relationships in Spain. But many volunteers' wartime correspondence makes plain that they did not go to Spain to fight, and in many cases die, for communism. They fought for liberty, equality and fraternity – the same Enlightenment Era ideals that inspired the French and American Revolutions. Their letters, coupled with the demonization of their idealism during the Cold War, also underscores how far the country had drifted away from the "spirit of 1776" and towards "blood and soil" the more it became the world's premier superpower in the second half of the twentieth century, and how imperialism changed the nature of American values.

www.ingramcontent.com/pod-product-compliance
Lightning Source LLC
Chambersburg PA
CBHW021155160426
43194CB00007B/748